T0131766

SORO SOKE

For the first time in human history, people aged over 65 now outnumber children under five. Yet one region in the world is bucking this trend: the world's top 20 youngest countries by population are all located in sub-Saharan Africa, and Africa's population under 35 now equals almost a billion people. While there has been much research and reportage in the West around the lives of Western millennials and Gen Z, little has been written on the dreams and aspirations, the fears and hopes, the needs and desires of young Africans. The Yoruba expression *Soro Soke*, meaning 'Speak Up', has become a clarion call for young Nigerians seeking to make their voices heard, and the phrase is resonating across the African continent and around the world via social media. Trish Lorenz speaks to the bright new entrepreneurs, artists and activists of Lagos and Abuja, Nigeria, to understand what it means to be young in an otherwise ageing world. This book is also available Open Access.

Trish Lorenz has been a journalist for more than 15 years. She is a regular contributor to titles including *The Guardian*, the *Financial Times* and *The Telegraph*, among others. Formerly a design columnist at *The Independent* and the Lisbon correspondent for *Monocle* magazine, she covers subjects ranging from design, art and culture to travel, politics and human interest pieces from around the world. In 2021, Trish was announced as the winner of the Nine Dots Prize.

TRISH LORENZ

SORO SOKE

THE YOUNG DISRUPTORS OF AN AFRICAN MEGACITY

CAMBRIDGE
UNIVERSITY PRESS

CAMBRIDGE
UNIVERSITY PRESS

University Printing House, Cambridge CB2 8BS, United Kingdom

One Liberty Plaza, 20th Floor, New York, NY 10006, USA

477 Williamstown Road, Port Melbourne, VIC 3207, Australia

314–321, 3rd Floor, Plot 3, Splendor Forum, Jasola District Centre,
New Delhi – 110025, India

103 Penang Road, #05–06/07, Visioncrest Commercial, Singapore 238467

Cambridge University Press is part of the University of Cambridge.

It furthers the University's mission by disseminating knowledge in the pursuit of
education, learning, and research at the highest international levels of excellence.

www.cambridge.org
Information on this title: www.cambridge.org/9781009211857
DOI: 10.1017/9781009211840

First published 2022

Revised June 2022

A catalogue record for this publication is available from the British Library.

ISBN 978-1-009-21185-7 Paperback

CONTENTS

FIGURES AND ILLUSTRATIONS

ABOUT THE NINE DOTS PRIZE

The Nine Dots Prize is unique in the world of literary prizes: it is an anonymously judged prize for a book that does not exist – yet.

Each cycle the Board sets a question about one of the big issues of our times, and we invite responses to that question in the form of a 3,000-word essay. The writer of the most compelling response receives $100,000, a book deal from Cambridge University Press, and support from the team at the Centre for Research in the Arts, Social Sciences and Humanities (CRASSH) at Cambridge University – i.e. everything they need to develop their response into a full-length book.

Crucially, the Prize is judged anonymously, on the strength of the essay and the supporting book outline alone. The Board doesn't receive any background information about entrants and any potentially identifying information is removed from the essays before judging begins. This is an attempt at levelling the playing field so that new and emerging thinkers have as good a chance of winning as established voices, regardless of their background, identity or career history.

The name of the Prize comes from the famous lateral thinking puzzle – in which nine dots need to be connected using four straight lines and without lifting the pencil from the paper – as it sums up what we were hoping to find: outside-of-the-box thinking.

In 2020, for the third cycle of the Prize, we posed the question 'What does it mean to be young in an ageing world?' We were delighted by the hundreds of submissions we received and the range of approaches entrants had taken, but there was one that stood out above all others. This entry made a thoroughly compelling and well-evidenced argument that the question of what it means to be young in the 21st century must not overlook the substantial youth populations of sub-Saharan African as they will play a significant role in shaping our world in the coming decades. Focusing on Nigeria – one of the youngest countries in the world, where more than 42 per cent of the population is under 14 years old – the entrant proposed conducting in-depth interviews with the youth population to explore the question using first-hand testimony. The Board was fully convinced by the argument and the rigour of the proposed approach. We were very pleased to announce Trish Lorenz as our winner and to follow her progress as she conducted the interviews that shaped this fascinating, vibrant and carefully researched book, *Soro Soke: The Young Disruptors of an African Megacity*.

Trish Lorenz follows in the footsteps of our first two winners, tech strategist turned Oxford philosopher, James Williams, and writer and journalist, Annie Zaidi.

Williams responded to the inaugural question 'Are digital technologies making politics impossible?' The resulting book, *Stand Out of Our Light: Freedom and Resistance in the Attention Economy*, was published in May 2018 to critical acclaim ('pay your full, undivided attention to this short, absorbing, and deeply disturbing book' – *Financial Times*) and chosen as Princeton University's 2019 Pre-read, sent to all incoming students as an introduction to intellectual life at Princeton. Zaidi's 'powerful' and 'unique' answer to the question 'Is there still no place like home?' became *Bread, Cement, Cactus: A Memoir of Belonging and Dislocation*, described by *The Observer* as a 'compelling exploration of the intimate and political sides of an itinerant life'.

As Trish Lorenz joins our list of winners and we see her book make its way into the world, we hope that readers will continue to follow the Prize as we seek to spark thoughts, discussion and debate about the most important questions of our times.

Professor Simon Goldhill
*Professor of Greek Literature and Culture
and Fellow of King's College, Cambridge
and Chair of the Nine Dots Prize Board*

For more about the Nine Dots Prize please visit ninedotsprize.org

1 THE SORO SOKE GENERATION

The world's people are getting old. According to the United Nations Population Fund (UNFPA), in 2018, for the first time in history, people aged over 65 outnumbered children under five. Europe has the greatest percentage of people over 60 (25 per cent) but rapid ageing is occurring almost everywhere: by 2100, the world will see just one birth for every octogenarian.[1] In most parts of the globe, we are moving into a time when there will be more elderly care homes than kindergartens, more funerals than celebrations of birth.

But there is one area that is bucking this trend: the world's 20 youngest countries by population are all situated in sub-Saharan Africa.[2] By 2050, Africa will be home to one billion young people,[3] while the number of young people in Europe is expected to shrink by 21 per cent and in Asia by almost a third.[4] As a result, by 2100 almost half of the world's youth are expected to be from Africa, and the continent's share of the global population is projected to grow from roughly 17 per cent in 2017 to around 40 per cent by 2100.[5] The UN's *World Population Prospects* says: 'In all plausible scenarios of future trends, Africa will play a central role in shaping the size and distribution of the world's population over the next few decades.'[6]

Dr Frank Swiaczny is a population specialist. A senior research fellow at the Federal Institute for Population Research in Germany and former assistant director at the United Nations Population Division in New York, he's been studying the world's demographics for more than two decades. Dr Swiaczny says that Africa's high youth

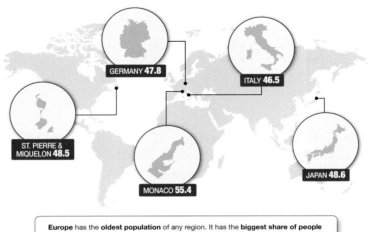

Europe has the oldest population of any region. It has the biggest share of people aged 60 and older, the smallest share of children under 15 and a median age of 43 years. That's almost 12 years older than the global median. With a median age of 39, Northern America is the second oldest region worldwide. By contrast, the median age across sub-Saharan Africa is 18.

Figure 1 Countries with the oldest average population age
Sources: www.statista.com/statistics/264727/median-age-of-the-population-in-selected-countries/ (2021) and Pew Research (2020) www.Pewresearch.org/fact-tank/2020/04/22/populations-skew-older-in-some-of-the-countries-hit-hard-by-covid-19/
Created by Russell Henry Design

population could trigger a raft of economic and social benefits for the continent – an outcome known as a demographic dividend.

'There is no doubt that the African continent will be completely different in future', he says. 'Most of the world's population growth is happening in sub-Saharan Africa and most of it will take place in cities. Africa should be in a phase of reaping a demographic dividend – a time when the population structure contributes to economic growth. This is the same dividend that South Korea and other Asian nations were able to harness in the 20th century, but it requires development in education, rule of law, democracy and gender equality.'

Percentage of world populations aged 65 or over, 2020

Percentage of world populations aged 65 or over, projected 2050

Figures 2 and 3 With the exception of sub-Saharan Africa, by 2050 most regions of the globe will have a quarter or more of their populations aged over 60
Source: United Nations, DESA, Population Division. *World Population Prospects 2019.* http://population.un.org/wpp/

Some of that dividend is already becoming evident. Dr Morten Jerven is Professor in Development Studies at the Norwegian University of Life Sciences. His 2015 book *Africa: Why Economists Get It Wrong* shows that most African economies have been growing at a rapid pace since the mid-1990s. He has written a follow-up book, *The Wealth and Poverty of African States* (2022), which uses tax receipts, wage data and historical GDP figures to further analyse African states. 'I believe empirical evidence will support the argument that failed African economies are a misnomer', he says.

A 2016 McKinsey Global Institute report, *Lions on the Move II: Realizing the Potential of Africa's Economies*, supports Jerven's view. It highlighted that growth across much of Africa accelerated to 4.4 per cent between 2010 to 2015. In 2016, Africa was already home to 700 companies with annual revenue of more than US$500 million, including 400 with annual revenue above US$1 billion. These companies, says the report, 'are growing faster and are more

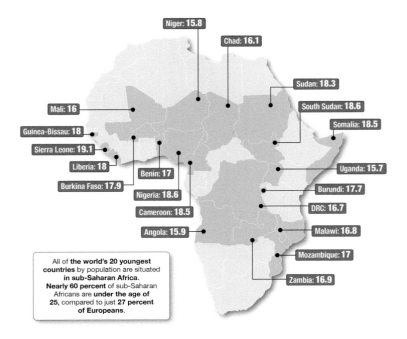

Figure 4 Top 20 countries with youngest average population age
Source: https://stacker.com/stories/2545/countries-youngest-and-oldest-
populations using data from the CIA World Factbook (2020) and US Census
Bureau International Database (2020)
Created by Russell Henry Design

profitable than their global peers'.[7] The report also notes that by 2034, Africa will have a larger working-age population than either China or India, which, when added to its abundant natural resources, acts as a signifier for future growth.

But despite the continent's growing economic power and the scale of its emerging youth cohort, both of which are likely to make a significant contribution to worldwide development in the 21st century, Africa remains a blind spot for most in the Global North. This generation of young sub-Saharan Africans, a rapidly growing population that will vastly outnumber their Western peers by 2050, are the leaders, the scientists, the artists and the entrepreneurs that will shape our world in the next 50 years and beyond. But, in the West at least, little is known of the fears and hopes, the dreams and aspirations of this youthful population. To date, most existing research around young people has been geared towards understanding Western millennials and Gen Z. Young Africans have been largely ignored or denigrated.

When the UNFPA's analysis of this emerging cohort was first released in 2014,[8] a *New York Times* discussion of the report was headlined 'The World Has a Problem: Too Many Young People'.[9] The newspaper's analysis concluded that 'the youth bulge stands to put greater pressure on the global economy, sow political unrest, spur mass migration and have profound consequences for everything from marriage to Internet access to the growth of cities'.

This regressive view, largely based on ignorance and a mix of systemic racism combined with post-colonial conceptions of superiority, is not unusual in the Global North. 'Sub-Saharan Africa has more variation than the EU, but we often talk about it as a whole, rather than study individual countries', says Dr Jerven. 'And at the moment, the main purpose of research still seems to be "what's wrong with Africa?" With demographics for example, it's more about European concerns rather than African potential. It's very us versus them.'

***

The opening sequence of the Marvel movie *Black Panther* moves from the poverty of Oakland, one of the more deprived cities in the US, to the thriving metropolis of Birnin Zana, the fictional capital of the fictional African country Wakanda.

Ostensibly, *Black Panther* tells the story of Wakanda's king and his fight for power but it also projects, perhaps for the first time in the history of Hollywood, a new vision of Africa. In the movie, Wakanda is far more developed than its Western counterparts, across everything from medicine and weaponry to gender equality. Its hospitals can cure wounds that would be fatal in the West; its weapons and armour are so superior that Western criminals attempt to steal them; and its women play a powerful role, running the armed forces and designing high-tech equipment.

In its depiction of an African country as advanced and sophisticated, *Black Panther* challenges traditional Western perspectives of the continent. Africa has been subject to profoundly damaging misconceptions since white foreigners first encountered it. Slavery and subjugation, the carving up of an entire continent without the consent of its peoples, the imposition of imperial borders based on nothing more than the political expediency of European powers set up a historic legacy more damaging than anywhere else on the globe. Africa's myriad peoples and cultures have long been dismissed or disregarded in the Global North. Across literature, film, news and even academia, the continent is almost invariably portrayed as poor and bereft of both history and opportunity. In 1963, Oxford historian Hugh Trevor-Roper infamously argued that Africa had no history prior to European exploration and colonisation: 'The rest is darkness ... the unedifying gyrations of barbarous tribes in picturesque but irrelevant corners of the globe', he wrote.[10]

This vision of Africa is a white creation, initially politically useful in justifying plunder and colonialism and more recently to enable a more subtle, but no more benign, Western dominance. It was never a true vision of the continent, and, as this book will show, it is certainly dated and myopic today. Wakanda offers a welcome counter-perspective. As Jelani Cobb writes in his *New Yorker* piece: 'Black Panther and the invention of "Africa"': 'No such nation as Wakanda exists on the map of the continent, but that is entirely beside the point. Wakanda is no more or less imaginary than the Africa conjured by [David] Hume or Trevor-Roper, or the one canonized in such Hollywood offerings as "Tarzan".'[11]

In fact, Wakanda reflects a nascent reality. Despite the enslavement of the continent's people, the destruction of its cultures and the ignorance and racism that persists to this day, African nations are thriving and growing. Inspiration for Wakanda could have come from Ghana, Kenya, Nigeria, Rwanda or South Africa – countries rich in educated, tech-enabled young talent entirely at home conceiving and developing solutions for a 21st-century world. And Birnin Zana, with its futuristic skyscrapers, racing trains and bustling street life, could be modelled on a host of African cities – the likes of Accra, Kigali or Lagos, the vast, energetic and flourishing commercial hub of Nigeria.

Often called the Giant of Africa, Nigeria is home to one in six sub-Saharan Africans and is currently the seventh most populated country in the world. Its population is projected to surpass that of the United States shortly before 2050, at which point it will be the world's third largest country.[12] Its borders, a product of British colonial convenience rather than any reflection of the ethnic make-up of the country, encompass three major tribes – the Yoruba, Igbo and Hausa – along with more than 200 smaller ethnic groupings. It is almost equally divided between two major

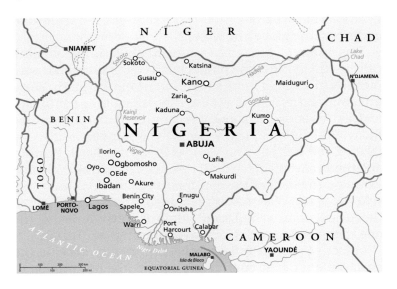

Figure 5 Map of Nigeria
Source: Shutterstock

religions: the Christian south and Muslim north. The country faces significant security challenges including Boko Haram terrorists in the north, Biafran calls for secession in the south-east, and banditry and competing interests for land use across large swathes of the interior. With the added challenges of an economic recession and the growing impact of the climate crisis, the country's lawmakers face a powder keg of competing interests, which they are largely failing to contain.

But the picture is far from entirely bleak. *The Economist* calls the country 'the continent's most boisterous democracy'.[13] It is Africa's largest economy, generating a quarter of the continent's GDP[14] and three of sub-Saharan Africa's four fintech unicorns (start-ups valued at more than US$1 billion) are Nigerian. The *Financial Times* calls Nigeria 'the potential economic powerhouse of the continent' and says: 'The country has all the ingredients for success. A huge population gives

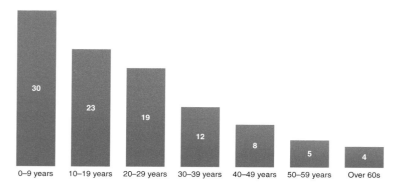

Figure 6 Percentage of Nigeria's population by age
Source: www.statista.com/statistics/1121317/age-distribution-of-population-in-nigeria-by-gender

it the scale other African economies lack. It is a coastal trading hub and the world's sixth-biggest oil exporter.'[15] It is also one of the youngest countries in the world: more than 42 per cent of Nigerians are under 14,[16] and half the population is under 19.[17] It is the only country among the world's five most populous that is forecast to have a rising working-age population for the rest of this century.[18]

***

The Nigerian writer and novelist Chinua Achebe is an important figure in modern African literature. In an interview with *Paris Review* magazine in 1994, he said: 'There is that great proverb – that until the lions have their own historians, the history of the hunt will always glorify the hunter. [Storytelling] is something we have to do, so that the story of the hunt will also reflect the agony, the travail, the bravery, even, of the lions.'[19]

This book aims to try to do just that. It documents the lives, ambitions, challenges and concerns of a group of young Nigerians living in the cities of Lagos and Abuja. It is their voices you will hear throughout the book – their hopes, their fears and their aspirations. By listening to these young Nigerians, by telling their stories, this book aims to reflect the dreams, the travails and the bravery of the young lions who will inherit the 21st century.

The young people you will meet in this book are, in the main, aged between 20 and 35. They are as different from their parents and grandparents as Western Gen Z are from Boomers. Although they share much in common with their Western counterparts, far more so than was the case a generation ago, they also inhabit a different world, with different challenges and different opportunities. And in talking with this cohort, a distinct generation emerges – creative, entrepreneurial, self-assured and hopeful, they are global in outlook but rooted in and proud of their Nigerian and African identity.

They also exhibit a confident outspokenness and a tendency for creative disruption. Enabled by the megacities in which they live and by access to technological advances – which together offer opportunities that were out of reach or simply did not exist for previous cohorts – this is a generation that is finding its voice and speaking out. This is the Soro Soke generation.

Soro Soke means 'speak up' in Yoruba, the language of the largest ethnic groups of Lagos and south-west Nigeria. (When correctly spelled, sọ̀rọ̀ sókè includes accents and tone marks. But, as the words have been co-opted as a protest slogan, the usage has simplified and it is this colloquial version that is used throughout the book.) The term first became a generational battle cry in the #endSARS youth protests against police brutality but has grown into the calling card of an entire cohort as it speaks up to demand opportunities and recognition. Whether it is calling out the economic challenges or failures in governance that are hampering its surge forward, celebrating its identity with vigour and pride or disrupting gender expectations and other social norms, the Soro Soke generation is making itself heard.

This book looks at two key factors that are shaping this cohort: urbanisation and technology. Urbanisation is changing the face of sub-Saharan Africa. By the end of this century, 13 out of 20 of the world's biggest cities will be concentrated on the continent.[20] Kinshasa, the capital of the Democratic Republic of Congo, is already the largest French-speaking city in the world (with Abidjan in Côte d'Ivoire and the Senegalese capital of Dakar, the third and fifth respectively). Lagos is sub-Saharan Africa's biggest conurbation and could be the world's biggest city by 2100,[21] as Greater Tokyo, currently the largest, looks set to shrink by almost a third due to an ageing population and declining birth rates.[22]

Cities shake things up: when people come together, creativity blossoms and innovation thrives; and Lagos is a vast metropolis with an economy significantly bigger than that of Kenya.[23] In the next chapter, young Lagosians discuss how life in the city is shaping them: they are emerging as a cohort of inventive problem solvers, filled with optimism and entrepreneurial drive.

Because of their diversity, megacities like Lagos also play an important role influencing cultural trends. The city's fashion industry is thriving, its music industry is having a global impact and the Nigerian film industry, known colloquially as Nollywood, makes more films than any other country, bar India.[24] For this generation, this explosion of creativity is rooted in expressing an African, as well as specifically Nigerian, identity. In Chapter 3, the Soro Soke generation talk about their pride in Nigerian and African culture and demonstrate how they are owning their heritage and spreading that message across the globe.

Religion and tradition still have a strong cultural hold in Nigeria, but some members of this younger cohort are

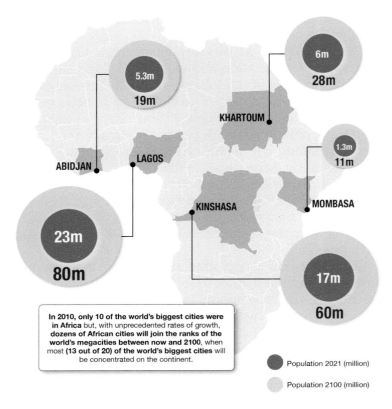

Figure 7 Predicted growth of five African cities by 2100
Source: www.washingtonpost.com/world/interactive/2021/africa-cities/
Created by Russell Henry Design

starting to speak up and confront social norms around gender identity and queerness. In Chapter 4, young Nigerians talk of how the increased wealth and cosmopolitan attitudes of city life, along with the burgeoning power of social media, are helping to give greater voice to marginalised groups.

Although urban life offers many opportunities, life in a developing megacity can also be a struggle. Emigration, the dream of a better life elsewhere, remains an aim for some, and in Chapter 5 the Soro Soke generation talk about the benefits and challenges of migration.

While increasing urbanisation plays a significant role in shaping young sub-Saharan Africans, it is access to technology that is perhaps the single greatest factor that differentiates this age group from those that came before. Technology is changing lives across the continent. As with their peers around the globe, new technologies are enabling the Soro Soke generation to mine opportunities that were unthinkable as little as a decade ago. This highly entrepreneurial cohort is using technology to leapfrog the Global North and turn intransigent pan-African problems into business opportunities that are both profitable and for the social good.[25] In Chapters 6 and 7, young Nigerians discuss how technology is changing their lives and highlight the freedom and entrepreneurial opportunities it offers them.

Social media also plays an outsize role. Access to social media is enabling young Nigerians to tell their own stories and engage on equal terms with those on the same platforms in the West. It has opened this generation to wider possibilities and viewpoints and is facilitating a growing recognition of what is no longer tolerable within their society, helping to create a generation that is both increasingly frustrated and willing to call out the injustices it faces. Young people are using social media to drive activism across the continent, such as the #endSARS movement against police brutality and corruption – discussed in Chapter 8 – which mobilised a generation in street protests across Nigeria.

One of the biggest challenges facing young sub-Saharan Africans is poor governance and access to power. Africa may be home to the youngest population on earth, but its leaders are among the oldest and often cling to power for decades. Nigeria is no exception: current president

Muhammadu Buhari is approaching 80 and is widely seen as out of touch with his young electorate. There is a recognition among the Soro Soke cohort that it has both the strength in numbers and the energy and ability to govern, but that it faces a real battle in accessing power. In Chapter 9, young activists in Abuja, the Nigerian capital, look to the future and discuss the issues and possible ways forward.

***

For some readers, particularly in the Global North, the stories in this book will be challenging. Encountering successful, strong, proud and outspoken young entrepreneurs, activists and leaders, there is an inclination to refute the relevance of their stories. Brought up on a diet of bleak news around sub-Saharan Africa, some will argue that the voices in this book are not representative, that these are the lucky few, the privileged minority. It is true there are people facing great hardship on the continent and that overcoming poverty is an ongoing battle for many. But in the past 40 years the African middle class has tripled to more than 330 million people and that number is predicted to exceed a billion by 2060.[26] Consumer spending is rising too, by almost 4 per cent every year, to more than US$1.93 trillion in 2021.[27]

It is cities that are experiencing the greatest growth in wealth and almost half a billion young sub-Saharan Africans live in the region's cities. Even by the most conservative estimate, well over a hundred million of these young people are working, studying, founding businesses, succeeding, building their lives, creating a future. That means millions upon millions who are renting apartments, eating in restaurants, being entertained in clubs and bars. They are online, on social media, using smartphones and laptops. They are living 21st-century lives. The stories in this book reflect this growing reality.

With almost a billion young people on the continent, no book can be a definitive round-up of every experience, every dream, every reality. Just as it is not possible for young people in New York to speak for the entire US, let alone for the whole of the North American continent, neither can young, urban Nigerians represent every member of their generation across a diverse country and a vast and disparate continent. But as one of the largest and most diverse groups, they offer a valuable insight into the changing landscape of young Africa. And it is only by listening to their voices, documenting the lives and dreams of the people who will lead, inspire and build our mutual future that we can begin to understand what it means to be young in an otherwise ageing world.

2 THE NEW YORK OF NIGERIA

'My advice is always, do what you can to come to Lagos. If you are young and creative, get yourself to Lagos. Lagos is the New York of Nigeria. Sometimes you don't know who you can be until you see it expressed somewhere else. I saw my first ever fashion show in Lagos. The year I moved to Lagos, Steve Wozniak came to give a talk. I got to listen to him and meet him. That would only happen in Lagos – Steve Wozniak isn't going anywhere else in Nigeria. You can do anything in Lagos. There are collectives geared around whatever your interest is. There's even a salsa dancing community. I went with a friend once and I couldn't believe it: salsa dancing here! There were a couple of Argentinians and Brazilians but really it was all Nigerians, all salsa dancing. Being in Lagos alters the way you see the world. Things are closer. You begin to think: I can do these things. You begin to figure out your place in the world from Lagos. You can do anything in Lagos. It's not easy, there's a lot of hustle and a higher cost of living but it's the place where you stand the highest chance.' John, 34

'There is almost a living energy here. Everyone you meet is running a business, running a side business, pushing forward every day, hustling. There are people on the road at 5am heading to work; there are people still on the road at 11pm heading back home. It's one of those cities in the world that doesn't pause. Lagos doesn't stop. It just continues. It's tough. It's hard. It's gritty. But everyone from all over the country is drawn to Lagos. Imagine what New York would be like if

San Francisco, Los Angeles, Washington DC, all the other big cities in the US, didn't exist and everyone just headed to New York. That's Lagos.' Odunayo, 28

'I like Nina Simone. Do you know her song "Young, Gifted and Black"? That's us. The young African in Lagos right now is excited. We live in this really terrible place. If you have a liveability index, Lagos is almost always the worst. Lagos does not work for anybody. It's terrible but so, so good as well. You have people doing the wildest things with nothing here. If you look across every sector, there are young people doing things. Even governance, as bad as it is, underneath the elected officials are a bunch of really efficient young people who are trying to change things. It's the people that make Lagos, the people who are innovating themselves out of this nightmare. That's not to say bad things don't happen here – they do – but it is exciting times. Oooouuuf! You know that cliché, that what doesn't kill you makes you stronger? Well, boy are we strong. Being a part of this generation feels like a gift. It's exciting, it's inspiring. There are not enough words.' S. I., 25

***

From the air, the city is a vast carpet of brown and green squares sewn together by silver grey stitching. The carpet stretches to the horizon, on and on and out of sight. As the plane drops lower, details emerge: rooftops and gardens become visible and the stitches morph into roads and acquire colour – the metallic tones of millions of vehicles reflecting the sunlight. The plane skims over homes, warehouses, a bustling market, a highway jammed with traffic and lands beside a sliver of green. Outside, the air is thick and heavy in the tropical heat and palm trees shiver in the breeze. An egret flies low, a white silhouette against the grass. On the streets, dense with traffic, cars spill messily across the lanes, trucks belch exhaust fumes. Small yellow Danfo – the minibuses that are endemic to Lagos and which traverse every corner of the city – pick up passengers, their conductors hanging precariously from the doorways. Auto-rickshaws, called *kekes*, toot and squeeze by, turning three lanes to four then five. Through the open window, the scent of sweet donuts and grilling meat emanating from roadside food stands mixes with the heady flavour of exhaust fumes. Slowly the vehicles edge forward and after a time the road becomes a long bridge straddling a wide lagoon, the water flecked with the gold and pink of the setting sun. Lights come on in the high glass office buildings on the island beyond the bridge and the skyline of a modern city emerges from the dusk.

Off the bridge and into evening life. Office workers in skirts and heels, some wearing brightly coloured *gele* – cloth headwraps that cover the hair – walk confidently along the sidewalk, avoiding potholes and scorning the traffic. Young men, many wearing traditional suits – slim-cut trousers topped with tunic-like jackets in

Figure 8 Lagos
Source: Michael Kraus/EyeEm/Getty Images

brightly patterned fabrics – lean in groups against walls, chatting and laughing. A man pushes a barrow filled with tomatoes; another sells cold drinks from a large pail. Tall and regal, these entrepreneurs, students, secretaries and fly boys, strong men and proud women, have the bearing of queens and princes. The overwhelming majority are young and all emanate confidence, panache and energy.

Welcome to Lagos, Nigeria. With a population of more than 20 million[1] it is one of the world's great megacities, as thriving and energetic as Bangkok and Hanoi, as sprawling and unequal in wealth and opportunity as São Paulo or Miami, and as full of dreams and aspirations as New York or London.

***

The pace of urbanisation across sub-Saharan Africa over the last 60 years is without precedent. In 1950, most African countries were agrarian societies and just over

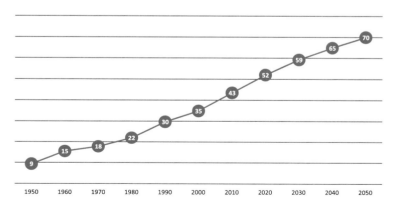

Figure 9 Growth of Nigeria's urban population, 1950–2050
Source: UN DESA World urbanisation prospects 2018, https://population.un.org/wup/Download

a quarter of the population lived in cities. By 2020, the continent had 74 cities with a population of more than one million people, equivalent to the US and Europe combined.[2] Today almost half of sub-Saharan Africans are urban dwellers and by 2050 that number is projected to reach 60 per cent. In the next 30 years, Africa will need to accommodate almost 950 million new urban dwellers, which is equivalent to what Europe, the US and Japan combined have managed over the last 265 years.[3] That means two-thirds of the continent's projected population growth over the next three decades will be absorbed by the region's humming, thriving, bustling megacities.[4] And, as the OECD notes, 'this transition is profoundly transforming the social, economic and political geography of the continent'.[5]

Those most impacted by the continent's growing urbanisation are the young. While historically it was rural to urban migration that contributed to the urban growth, today it is largely due to natural population increase. The Soro Soke generation are the children of cities and this is changing their life prospects, their mindset and their cultural expression.

The growth of megacities has led to a density and connectivity previously unseen in Africa, which remains physically fragmented due to poor infrastructure. Cities like Lagos give young people access to jobs and entrepreneurial opportunities, create income and growth and, by their density, enable a leap forward in the ability to innovate. Evidence suggests that doubling a city's size boosts income per capita between 3 and 8 per cent.[6] Lagos confirms the opportunities cities bring – it has a nominal per capita income of more than US$5,000, more than double the Nigerian average.[7] The city is home to a pan-African banking industry, it is a leader in the fintech and cryptocurrency sectors and has become one of the continent's biggest tech hubs.

'In terms of spirit of opportunity, Lagos is the epicentre', says 30-year-old entrepreneur Davies Okeowo. 'People come here, from across the country and other places because they think "if I put in the effort, I will make it work". If you really work, it really is possible. The optimism in the tech space is typical. The start-up eco-system is crazy in Lagos. We have a number of unicorns already and a lot more are going to come. Capital is continuing to flow, and it is much better from an economic standpoint.'

Odunayo Eweniyi, 28, is a tech company founder and CEO. Her company, PiggyVest, which she co-founded when she was 22, has three million customers and is credited with changing the way young Nigerians save and invest. 'There are a lot of problems in Lagos but it's also one of the best places in Nigeria for entrepreneurship', she says. 'It's only in Lagos where three people, like myself and my co-founders, could come, start a company and have people trusting us. All industry is here, everyone from all over the country is drawn to Lagos.'

The Yaba district, which includes the busy, vibrant neighbourhood of Ojuelegba immortalised in the Wiz-Kid song of the same name, is the tech centre of the city. Colloquially known as Yabacon Valley because of its predominance of start-ups, it is home to a host of small tech campuses featuring bright contemporary branding and the kind of young, hip workforce that wouldn't be out of place in San Francisco. The streets are filled with a cacophony of cars, Danfo buses and motorcycle taxis. Vibrant clubs pumping Afrofusion beats sit beside bars and takeaway restaurant chains that appeal to a youthful audience of developers, entrepreneurs and creatives.

'I was drawn in by the promise of the city, but I moved here for the people most of all', says influencer and entrepreneur John Obidi, 34. 'The people are creative, hopeful and full of promise. They are Nigerian thought leaders making an impression on a global scale. All

Nigeria's great creatives are based in Lagos, and they pushed me to achieve, too.'

Yaba illustrates the opportunity that African cities have to reshape urban thinking, moving away from what American research group the Brookings Institution calls 'lumpy grid infrastructure'[8] and towards a more flexible way of living that utilises technology, peer-to-peer transactions and entrepreneurial energy to create a successful, liveable and productive city.

'Yaba has a great support system – if you are looking for a writer, or a programmer or a designer you can find one here. And Lagos was one of the first cities in Nigeria to have creative hubs like Co-Creative Hub in Yaba', says Obidi. 'CCH is a co-working space with good internet access and running electricity and other people who are there for the same purpose. To have access to that office space, to be able to work there with all the facilities and brilliant people was amazing. I remember being there as great days – working together, sharing ideas, creating creative synergies. And the crop of creatives I worked with, we forged relationships and many of them have gone on to do great things all over the world.'

Yaba is situated on mainland Lagos, near to the thriving university district of UniLag and not far from middle-class neighbourhoods such as Ikeja. The 12km-long Third Mainland Bridge connects these districts to the upmarket island suburbs and the up-and-coming Lekki Peninsula. In wealthy island neighbourhoods like Banana Island and Ikoyi, huge homes, palatial in scale, sit behind high walls that hide large gardens complete with swimming pools and tennis courts. The Eko Atlantic development on Victoria Island is an entire sub-city overlooking the ocean and targeting the super wealthy. (Eko is the original Bini language name for the Lagos region.) This new 25sq km peninsula, reclaimed from what was formerly a popular public beach, is designed to be home to 250,000 residents

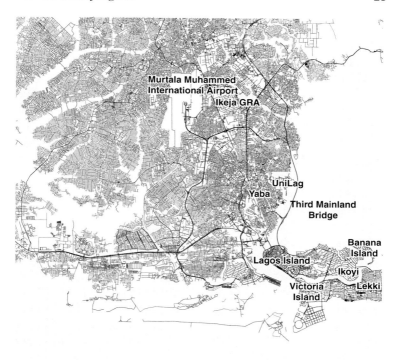

Figure 10 Map of Lagos mainland and islands
Source: Getty Images

and accommodate a daily flow of 150,000 commuters. But the site stands mostly empty, just two towers of luxury apartments are marooned in one corner of the huge site.

Olamide Udoma-Ejorh, 36, is executive director at the not-for-profit Lagos Urban Development Initiative (LUDI). She believes luxury developments like Eko Atlantic have had their time. 'The last two administrations in Lagos had a vision of the city that was all about grand gestures that look glossy but are not really helping anybody. Take Eko Atlantic. It has become so upscale that even the rich can't afford it and you can see they are not really building.

Recently I've noticed a real shift in thinking – it's more about how we can do something to help the population', she says.

Cities are catalysts for economic growth, innovation and employment but are also more unequal than rural areas.[9] As is the case in most cities around the world, wealth in Lagos is unevenly distributed. Slow growth and two recessions have made Nigerians poorer, on average, each year since oil prices fell in 2015, and bad central government decisions have led to the devaluation of the currency and seen annual food inflation soar above 20 per cent – a major issue in a country where many people live on less than US$1 a day.[10] Lagos is richer than most Nigerian regions. According to the country's National Bureau of Statistics (NBS), 4.5 per cent of the population of Lagos state were living below the poverty line in 2020 – the country's lowest percentage.[11] But in a city of 20 million this is still a large number of people, and Lagos has several neighbourhoods, the likes of Makoko, where housing is makeshift and temporary and severe deprivation and extreme poverty are rampant. There is a desperate shortage of affordable housing across the city, and, for the slightly better-off working poor, *face-me-I-face-you* housing, where several people sleep in the same room, remains common, particularly among young men.

Young local architects, such as Baba Oladeji, 32, are now challenging conventional thinking to try to build a city that also works for its poorer inhabitants. Oladeji's practice, Ministry of Architecture, fuses politics with architecture and seeks to rethink post-colonial African cities. 'In Nigeria it is very common that you have people living day to day', he says. 'When you are poor, you can't plan long term, you simply cannot. You plan day by day how to survive. Our economic systems and built environment should reflect that. It's frustrating that African governments are still intent on urbanising within the parameters of the West because the idea of a mortgage or a shopping mall are flawed ideas here. We need a theory of impermanence and informality. These are concepts we should embrace. In my practice, we try to consider the informal structures that reflect how we live our lives – umbrella markets, temporary dwellings, hawkers on the move among traffic.'

Oladeji is working on a project in the north of the country creating temporary dwellings for displaced persons. 'We are doing what local people are already doing but making it stronger', he says. 'We use bamboo frames that can be decommissioned and zinc roofing sheets, a material that is abundant in Nigeria. I find beauty in it, the language of rust.'

He is hoping that learnings from the project can be applied in Lagos to offer poor young people access to the property market. 'In the 1960s you could afford to buy a house in Lagos. Today you can't. We want to find a piece of land, close to the city centre, so young people can have proximity to work and own their own asset. We have a chance to diversify away from standard global real estate stock, to move away from the idea of permanence to the semiotics of impermanence. We'd be able to match the price of rent and build a home for young people who are a part of the urban poor.'

Affordable housing is one big issue in Lagos; traffic congestion is another – at 67 minutes in each direction, the city has the highest average commuting time in the world (above San José in Costa Rica (64 minutes), Colombo (62), Los Angeles (61) and Calcutta (60)).[12] Images of its blocked roads have become iconic, and traffic jams leave its residents scarred and embattled. There are as many strategies for avoiding its stranglehold as there are drivers. And everyone drives here: estimates suggest there are five million cars on the road each day, with around eight million passengers in them.[13]

Roads in Lagos are largely paved, there are wide bridges holding three or four lanes of traffic in each direction to link the mainland to the islands, and effective and well-made toll roads have helped ease congestion somewhat. But on a working day in Lekki, an increasingly popular suburb on a long, thin peninsula bordered by the Gulf of Guinea to the west and the waters of the city's vast lagoon on the east, the traffic remains snarled and moody. Car after car is jammed across the three lanes of the main road that runs like a spine along the many miles of the peninsula. Horns tooting, hands gesticulating, bumpers brushing, the vehicles sputter along.

For some, the city's perennial traffic has become just one more entrepreneurial opportunity. Hawkers, on foot, walk the lines of semi-stationary vehicles, selling everything

Figure 11 For some, the city's perennial traffic has become an entrepreneurial opportunity
Source: Oluwafemi Dawodu/Shutterstock

from cold drinks to peanuts, throw pillows, hats and vividly coloured paintings. One hawker holds shower caddies, another hedge clippers. Others sell drain cleaners, wallets, face masks, wall clocks, games, paintings, jewellery, books or windscreen wipers.

Funmi Oyatogun, 29, is the founder of travel firm TVP Adventures. She's been leading tour groups across Nigeria and Africa since 2016 and calls herself 'Africa's most adventurous woman'. It's her ambition to visit every country in the world, but today she is closer to home, taking a guided tour of Lagos. 'We say that you can furnish your home or buy dinner and the implements to cook it, while you're stuck in traffic', says Oyatogun, laughing.

Despite the prevalence of cars, more than 12 million Lagosians also use public transport services daily.[14] The informal yellow Danfo buses form part of Lagos' cultural identity,[15] but a formal working infrastructure of public transport is missing. There are no trains, no trams, no metro. Lagos is not Nigeria's capital. Since 1991, that designation has belonged to Abuja, some 600km to the north, a purpose-built city that is home to the country's political elite. When the new capital was pronounced, the nation's revenues began a commensurate flow, away from Lagos and towards the north. Despite being the country's largest city, Lagos has suffered from a lack of infrastructure investment ever since.

'There is a transport master plan. It is quite old, 10 years maybe, and it does include trains, elevated railways and other public transport', says Udoma-Ejorh. 'There is some progress, but the city is quite slow at achieving it.'

With the population of Lagos growing rapidly, there is an urgent need to make it more liveable. Public spaces like parks are rare. Bicycle lanes and bicycle traffic are non-existent, even walking is a challenge – well-defined sidewalks are few, making walking an extreme sport of dodging traffic while sidestepping puddles and potholes.

Udoma-Ejorh believes a focus on large infrastructure projects to the exclusion of improvements at a community level is part of the problem. 'The government's push is on larger infrastructure rather than smaller changes that could improve community living', she says. 'I think the state also needs to think about layers of the city and how people move through the city at different times. We need more than just large infrastructure. We also need smaller interventions at a micro level.'

Her young team at LUDI works to improve local areas – the organisation is creating vertical gardens and farms, new parks and public spaces and focusing on enabling non-motorised traffic and improving pedestrian safety. 'Most of our projects are around transportation and mobility, particularly non-motorised transport. We also look at public space, climate resilience and building a more equitable city. We have a pro-poor ethos', says Udoma-Ejorh.

Taking personal action to solve larger problems is one of the traits that defines the Soro Soke generation. Sometimes, as with LUDI, it's a proactive engagement. In other cases, it is because there is no other choice. 'Nigerians can solve any problem you give them', says Oyatogun. 'We have to be able to, no one is coming to solve it for us.'

A large truck is slowing progress on the Lekki toll road, the sides of its tanks seeping liquid and leaving spotted trails on the road behind. It is a water tanker, a common sight on roads throughout the city. Neither water nor electricity can be taken for granted in Lagos. Electricity flutters in and out, a sudden drop into darkness elicits no comments here. Those who can afford it run their own generators. But it is water supply that is the more pressing issue. The city's creaking water facility can't meet modern needs and many Lagosians have resorted to trucking water in, or to drilling their own wells. But as more people drill deeper and deeper, the underground water reservoir is being depleted. Lagosians acknowledge the need for governance on the issue but are also resigned to managing alone.

'I have to care for myself', says 25-year-old journalist S. I. Ohumu. 'We all know what it is to not have water, or not to have electricity. Only a very few very wealthy Nigerians haven't had a similar experience. It's the young people in Lagos and other cities who are innovating themselves out of this nightmare. We don't have an option. You have to get ahead yourself, and you have to take as many people as possible ahead with you.'

Across Lagos, young Nigerians are gathering in like-minded groups. Whether it is solving problems of urban planning, building business to help each other save and invest, making music and having fun or standing up for each other against police and government forces, young Lagosians are inspiring each other and working together to solve the challenges they face. In the process they are creatively disrupting both the cityscape and traditional life. In her paper 'Youth in Angola: Keeping the Pace towards Modernity', Cristina Udelsmann Rodrigues points out that, across Africa, urban modes of living are generating new forms of social and cultural interaction. Young people, she says, are eager to distinguish themselves from the rural past and develop new, cosmopolitan styles. 'In clothing and fashion, places where people eat, urban leisure and the transformation of gender relationships, among others, the construction of new social and cultural references and practices shows how active the role of younger generations is, and how they are able to contribute to the transformation of society', writes Rodrigues.[16]

The GRA (Government Residential Area) of Ikeja epitomises the modernity of thinking and living that is evident in many parts of Lagos. An area of detached houses and apartments in gated communities, it attracts civil servants and business people of all ages. Many of its residents are young and successful – this is where Oyatogun lives. 'It's quiet here, peaceful', she says, a rare feeling in this teeming city.

Like many residents, she values the neighbourhood's proximity to the airport and its shopping malls, boutiques, supermarkets, restaurants, and the likes of the Hans & René gelato parlour, which serves ice cream with flavours such as Agbalumo (star apple). Hans & René is typical of an emerging side of Lagos – cosmopolitan yet rooted in Nigerian culture it appeals to a growing group of young people, those with jobs or businesses, who have money and want to spend it in support of a new, distinct, urban Nigerian lifestyle.

As Oladeji points out: 'The spirit of a city is very important, we inhabit the spirit of where we live. Lagos is very cosmopolitan, it is multiple cultures and multiple identities. It's complex, a melting pot of many things. I'm interested in the material aspect of our culture but also in the philosophical and I believe Nigerians don't yet fully realise how much the city influences our culture.'

SPEAKING OUT: CHEKWUBE OKONKWO ON EXPRESSING AFRICAN IDENTITY

'The concept of Africa in your head is different to the one that is in mine, so if I make it, you might not see it for what it is.'

Figure 12 Chekwube Okonkwo, 29, is the co-founder and art director at Lagos-based Magic Carpet Studios
Credit: Fati Abubakar

***

'Our culture is very rich in so many ways. It is so diverse, so many tribes, so many countries. We can't sum it up to one. Even in Nigeria, the southern Igbo culture is very different to the north. So where do you start from in defining African identity?

One thing that has summarised it all is abstraction. If you look at the woodwork and paintings from the past, you see they were not going for a realistic approach. They were trying to draw an image with simple lines. It's a very beautiful and sophisticated form of art. You wonder, from what realm were they getting this from? What I understand about the traditional process is that it is very spiritual. It's been said that they would go to a secret place to make these sculptures. They would pray to the wood, and so on.

What I say is, that works for us today, too. We should also look to ourselves. You don't start with the intention that you want to make African art; you start it by going to a secret place within yourself, spending time, digging down and something will birth. I do a lot of research, I do a lot of reading of African literature and away from reading, I just look around a lot. I try to see the world around me. The truth is that times have changed, and this should reflect in the art. Good art tells of the time and season in which it's made – it is not in the costuming or African attire or pattern.

A lot of people have come to me and asked me: How do we make it ours? There is a way that we use colours, the colours are just so rich, so perhaps that's something. The colour of our skin, too, gives it an African identity.

But really, the question is not how to make it ours. The question is: If I make it, are you open enough to accept it? What is the concept of Africa in your own head? The concept of Africa in your head is different to the one that is in mine, so if I make it, you might not see it for what it is.'

3   CULTURAL CAPITAL

'More and more people are getting in touch with their African identity, especially the younger Gen Z. They are really into learning and discovery and I have so much hope in them. Personally, I want to tell actual Nigerian stories and I want to use our language to do it. In my screenplays I use Pidgin and local names and local languages. In the past I was often asked to change it but now that I'm doing my own work, I do it a lot.' Uyaiedu, 32

'The representation of books in Nigeria is not as culturally diverse as it should be. There are books written in Yoruba and other languages but when you walk into a bookstore you find mostly books written in English. There are some things you say that sound better in your mother tongue. I want to see more Nigerian books written in the traditional languages.' Oyindamola, 25

'African designers are beginning to express themselves; we are beginning to forge our own design style. I've seen people create a Danfo font, based on the yellow local buses that move around in Lagos. A friend in Zimbabwe has been looking at African patterns to discover the design language embedded in those patterns. It's really exciting.' Bolanle, 28

'Being an artist in Nigeria right now is great. I know a number of artists of my generation that are showing at art fairs outside the country. African artists, Nigerian artists are getting global attention. And it's not the older generation, it's the younger ones.' Osinachi, 30

'We are working on an animated TV series called Meet the
Igwes. *It is based on this part of the world, on Lagos. We
find our story lines and ideas through word on the street,
something catches our eye, or a rumour is making the rounds
on social media. Many of the characters are based on people
we know, especially supporting characters. I modelled one
character after the way one of my neighbours talks. I studied
the way he walks and talks, the way he sees the world. The
background and story is ours but we can pull from people we
meet.'* Isaac, 30

*'Five years ago, there was no one doing Nigerian cuisine.
Every Nigerian chef would be doing French food or American
food. It was foie gras this and caviar that. It was seen as giving you higher-level food. And then I came and said I'm not
going to use any ingredient that we don't grow in Nigeria.
And now people aren't making a differentiation anymore.
Before, the catch of the day was downgraded on the menu
and salmon, a fish we don't have close to our waters, was seen
as better. Today, we have fish that is good and that's what
we are serving. It's being driven by the younger generation. I
think the younger generation are educating the older generation on how to approach our culture generally.'* Michael, 32

***

Lagos has undergone a cultural transformation since the
turn of the century. Driven by its vast youth population,
its creative industries – from art and design to music, film
and fashion – are booming. *Vogue* magazine hails Lagos as
West Africa's cultural capital[1] and the *Financial Times* says:
'The city is home to a thriving music, fashion and film
scene that reverberates around the continent.'[2]

Nigeria's media and entertainment industry stands to
be one of its greatest exports. With a projected annual
growth rate of 8.6 per cent, it is one of the fastest growing
in the world.[3] The country's film industry, Nollywood, was

worth US$3.6 billion in 2016, and contributed 2.3 per cent, about 239 billion naira (US$660 million), to GDP in 2021.[4]

But it is the music industry that is most indicative of how the Soro Soke generation, influenced by life in a vast megacity, is upending and disrupting perceptions of Nigerian culture. According to the Nigerian Minister of Information and Culture, Lai Mohammed, the country's music industry will generate US$86 million (3.09 billion naira) in revenue in 2021, making it the region's largest.[5] In the past six years, a growing number of new production studios and artists have created a vibrant and self-sustaining industry and produced a string of world-class music that has won awards, fans and acclaim around the globe.

As Ikenna Emmanuel Onwuegbuna points out in his 2010 paper on African pop music, urbanisation has helped to create an entirely new sound.[6] 'This new social order differs widely from former homogeneous ethnic settings', writes Onwuegbuna. 'And in expressing their musical artistry, urban dwellers, drawn from different ethnic backgrounds, are creating a syncretic urban neo-folk music.'[7]

The music emanating from Lagos epitomises Onwuegbuna's view of syncretic expression. Drawing from a variety of influences and embracing a mix of musical styles, young Nigerian musicians are combining R&B, hip-hop, dancehall and traditional sounds to create an entirely new sound known as Afrofusion.[8] And rather than simply adapting global trends, they are embracing and amplifying their African identity.

Perhaps the most well-known proponents of the Afrofusion sound are Damini Ogulu, 31 (better known as Burna Boy), and Ayo Balogun, 32 (who performs as WizKid). On his 2011 debut album WizKid switches between English, Pidgin and Yoruba. Burna Boy incorporates languages such as Zulu and usually sings in a combination of Yoruba and English. Neither artist has diluted his Nigerian culture in a bid to appeal to a global audience, in fact, quite the opposite.

Figure 13 WizKid and Burna Boy perform at London's O2 stadium in December 2021
Source: Joseph Okpako/Getty Images

American rapper and producer Sean Combs, aka Diddy, calls Burna Boy's 2020 album *Twice as Tall* 'a modern but pure, unapologetic African body of work'.[9]

Ndeye Diagne is the West Africa managing director at consultancy and data analytics firm Kantar. In 2019, she headed up the company's Africa Life study, which surveyed 5,000 people in cities across six countries – Nigeria, Ghana, Kenya, Senegal, Côte d'Ivoire and Cameroon – with a follow-up survey of 3,500 across Nigeria, Kenya, Ghana, Senegal and South Africa in 2021.[10] The process involved an hour-long, face-to-face questionnaire across a statistically robust and nationally representative sample with questions covering values, aspiration, lifestyle, media consumption, technological uptake and consumer confidence. The studies highlight that the growing confidence and pride in African identity expressed by musicians like Burna Boy is reflective of a generation.

'This younger generation is very proud of their culture and all that comes with it', says Diagne. 'Pride and creativity in expressing their identity is a very big part of who they are. They create products that celebrate Africa, that use local elements, across music and fashion and more. They are determined to create a different future for Africa. To create an Africa that counts and that inspires the world.'

The Global North no longer resonates as the key tastemaker for this generation. They do not disregard it, but they do not prioritise it either. 'This generation are citizens of a boundless world but feel deeply rooted in their African culture', says Diagne. 'There is a growing confidence and pride in Africa. They are not closing themselves off from the rest of the world, in fact they are very open and are very creative in the way they blend heritage with Western influences. But they are grounded in who they are and in their African identity.'

Burna Boy epitomises the confidence, vision and anger that fire the Soro Soke generation. Along with using local languages and local melodies, his lyrics address social issues and misperceptions of Africa. He has said he believes it is important for Africa to be heard and that his music 'is building a bridge that leads every Black person in the world to come together'.[11] He talks often about the injustices of imperialism. 'They don't teach the right history, the history of strength and power that we originally had. They don't really teach the truth about how we ended up in the situation we're in', he said in a *New York Times* interview.[12] When the 2020 Grammy Award for world music went to long-established Beninese singer Angélique Kidjo, she dedicated her trophy to Burna Boy, praising him for 'changing the way our continent is perceived'.[13]

The success of Nigerian musicians also illustrates another important element of this generation's cultural output: the direction of influence is now much more egalitarian. African musicians have had international success in the past, the likes of Nigerian superstar Fela Kuti, Youssou N'Dour from Senegal and South African Miriam Makeba. But they were individual success stories and wider African musical genres had limited global impact. That has changed.

Burna Boy's *Twice as Tall* was nominated for the Best World Music Album at the Grammys, amassed over 11.4 million streams in the US in its first week and debuted at number 1 on Billboard's World Music Charts.[14] WizKid's 2021 London O2 arena tour of *Made in Lagos* sold out in minutes and his song 'Essence' became the first African song to go platinum in the US, where it sold more than one million copies. WizKid has collaborated with North American stars including Drake and Justin Bieber. Beyoncé is a Burna Boy fan, and he has also collaborated with British stars such as Sam Smith and Stormzy.

'In the past we were proud of our culture, but it was not so visibly expressed', says Diagne. 'All the power lay with the West, so Africanity was a bit suppressed. The difference today is that young people are more open and vocal about African identity, and it is seen as positive and exciting. In fact, now the Western world is tapping into it.'

This confidence and pride in local culture is a theme that extends beyond the music industry. Uyaiedu Ipke-Etim, 32, is a Lagos-based writer and film-maker who explores the use of local language in her work. 'Pidgin is often seen as a lower-class language', she says. 'At school we were punished for speaking Pidgin. It's a remnant of colonialism that you should speak the Queen's English. I say a big fuck you to that. We speak more flavourfully, and Pidgin expresses that.'

Chekwube Okonkwo, 29, and Isaac Matui, 30, are part of the young creative team that heads up Magic Carpet Studios, which creates animated films and television series – a first feature film, *The Passport of Mallam Ilia*, is currently in production. The studio is committed to exploring African stories in its work and this first film is an adaptation of a young adult Nigerian novel that is set in the country's Muslim north.

'There is something unique about northern Nigerian culture; it is so rich and so deep that we wanted to explore it artistically', says Okonkwo, the studio's co-founder and lead art director.

In adapting the work, Okonkwo and Matui, the studio's head of story, discovered and embraced a cultural difference in storytelling. 'Most animated films are about the happy ever after, show business type endings – people want to have a good time in the cinema. But I think we are just beginning to understand that if we want to tell African stories and tell them authentically, we have to be true about it', says Okonkwo. 'Our stories dive into the cause and effects of things. We don't really care about the plot – it's more about the moral of the story. This is typical to

Figures 14 and 15 Promotional poster and still from Magic Carpet's first feature film, *The Passport of Mallam Ilia*
Credit: Chekwube Okonkwo, co-founder and art director at Magic Carpet Studios

most African stories. How the character ends up, whatever quest she embarks on, it's all tied into that. I grew up with my father telling me stories, under the moonlight on our balcony. Some stories, I couldn't understand at the time but as you get older you get the gist of it. With our stories, kids grow to understanding.'

The challenge for some young artists and designers, now, lies in debunking Western myths and stereotypes around African culture. Speaking to *Vogue* magazine, Omoyemi Akerele, who launched Lagos Fashion Week, said: 'Sometimes there's a question if the aesthetic is not obviously African. If you don't see the print, you don't see the pattern, you don't see the embellishments. The question you get is, "Oh, is this an African brand?" It's about trying to tell them, "Listen, this designer might have a pared-down, almost minimalist influence, but that doesn't make them less African."'[15]

Okonkwo concurs with the sentiment. 'Sometimes you see animators and artists trying to Africanise their work. It might be set in the present day, but they put some beads or a calabash to make it African. But then it feels like Africa is becoming foreign to Africans. It becomes like a fictional world, a Wakanda-like world.'

This is not the way Magic Carpet works. The studio has big ambitions, but Matui is clear that it does not care to measure itself against studios in the West. 'We are not the Disney of Africa, we are the Magic Carpet of Africa', he says. 'We don't have to be under the shadow of anything. They started from somewhere and we are starting from somewhere too. At the end of the day, we want to build something here.'

To a very large degree, the Soro Soke generation has no truck with playing to Western narratives. This young cohort is finding its voice, identity and freedom in sincerity of expression.

'My generation has been dealt a very bad card economically; we've been forced to look within, to find this aspect of cultural awareness, identity awareness', says 32-year-old chef Michael Elégbèdé. 'We own who we are and how we express ourselves. I think we are finally understanding that ownership of our identity is freedom. We are demanding the freedom that we deserve. And part of that freedom is expressing our culture and who we are, in a way that is true to us.'

SPEAKING OUT: OSINACHI ON ART AND NIGERIAN IDENTITY

'I see contemporary art by Africans as a way of reclaiming what was lost.'

***

'I have always believed that art should serve other purposes aside from the aesthetic purpose. I mean it's beautiful when you hang the artwork in your space but there is the other question: What is

Figure 16 Osinachi, 30, is a digital visual artist based in Lagos. He has been described as 'Africa's foremost crypto artist' and is currently working on the theme of the relationship between art, Africa and its cultures.
Credit: Fati Abubakar

it saying and what is it contributing to society? I started paying attention to the effects of colonialism, one of which is the looting of cultural artefacts from Africa. I see contemporary art by Africans as a way of reclaiming what was lost.

Growing up in Aba, in eastern Nigeria, I don't think there were any galleries. Perhaps there were one or two but, growing up, I never heard about art galleries. I never heard about art shows. The only thing I was exposed to growing up were old photographs of my family. Old black and white photographs of when my dad was young, my mum was young, my grandmother. I knew through the Internet about visual art, so I just went ahead and started creating my thing. Recently, looking at a photo of my dad as a young man, I realised that I am reacting to these photos, that you can still see the influence of these photographs in my work.

I'm Nigerian before I'm African but my Igbo identity is the strongest. I call myself by my Igbo name, not my Western name, and sometimes I use Igbo words as the titles of my work. And sometimes I use the piece to interrogate my Igbo identity. If you look at a piece like In Touch, *the man standing with the leopard, that is what I did there.*

The Igbo people have a special relationship to the leopard, which is called agu *in our language. The leopard is extinct in Igboland now but in the past people were afraid of the leopard, yet they also hunted it, especially the men. Anyone who was able to kill a leopard would be called Ogbuagu: "Killer of leopard". It's a very big title to have in our culture.*

With colonialism, education stopped happening in the way that it should have. It is difficult for young people, even myself, to make a sentence in Igbo, without putting in an English word. Young people now use the word agu *for the lion. But in this part of the world, we don't have the lion, what we had was the leopard. It is still a conversation that young people need to have, of how we reclaim our language. There is this education that needs to happen because language is so important – one way we make sense of the world around us is through language.*

Art is another way to really make sense of your world and to share that experience with people. You are transacting culturally with art. We all come from a different culture. You give me your experience, I give you my experience, visually. And we keep adding to the beauty of the world, we keep adding to conversations around diversity and culture.'

SPEAKING OUT:
PRISCILLA EKE
ON FEMINISM

'It's a long-term battle but it starts now. We are speaking out more. We are calling things out. We are in the face of people we need to be in the face of.'

Figure 17 Priscilla Eke, 30, is a PhD researcher on Nigeria's gender gap in leadership
Credit: Priscilla Eke

***

'There is an idea that no matter your academic achievement, if you are not a wife and a mother then you haven't achieved anything. All my years, my degree, my career goals don't count for anything just because I'm a woman and I don't have a husband or kids. People are always asking, "Where is your husband? Are you talking to anyone?" A lady or an uncle will give you advice: all this means nothing if you are not married with kids. It's one of the criteria on which women are judged.

Even married women, decisions are made on their behalf. You can't make decisions on your own, your husband has the final say. Or they say: "We cannot give you certain jobs because it means that your earnings might be greater than your husband so we can't even consider you for certain positions."

In our history, if you go back to pre-colonial era, women were actually in charge of things, they were part of the community, had authority. We had women kings and women chiefs and women who held titles, who were in charge of different sectors within communities. But as you go through the colonial era it was the men that were sent to school, only the men, and power and access were given to men and the women were just sent back to the home. The culture now is not the culture of where we started from. We are holding on to Western culture, this wasn't really our culture.

Younger women understand that there are certain things that marginalise them in terms of their thinking about what they can do, and they are trying to change that whole narrative. It's a long-term battle but it starts now. We are speaking out more. We are calling things out. We are in the face of people we need to be in the face of. And dare I say, maybe we are a bit harsh and forceful but we are speaking up, we are questioning things and are getting people to stop and think. People in positions of power, people who are much older than us, people who have reproduced this culture we are in, we are getting them to stop and question and to think "ok, maybe I got it wrong, maybe there is a new and different way that you can do something".'

4   CHALLENGING NORMS

'Feminism in Nigeria is not a subject. There is this idea that it is Western ideology, that it goes against everything Nigerian culture stands for and if you support feminism you are trying to destabilise our whole culture. They use the word "feminist" as an insult. They throw the term at women, "oh, you're a feminist" and that means you never get married, never raise a family, you are here to destroy the society. Which of course we aren't. Feminism is about a better future for women, which equals a better society for everyone.' Priscilla, 30

'I don't think I'm anybody's role model but, whether you like it or not, as a woman who has managed to break the glass ceiling you have a responsibility to let more women in. To be honest I don't think diversity and inclusion is charity. It's really not. It's very profitable. It's economically sound to have women working. There is a balance that needs to be achieved and its very glaring when women are not there. I'm not asking you to hire women for women's sake – I'm asking you to better your organisation because balance is both progressive and profitable.' Odunayo, 28

'I got married almost a year ago; I met my husband in tech. We are in the house, both constantly on our laptops, both always working. He works in fintech, so he understands how it feels. We are not trying to make our lives difficult by saying "oh there are gender roles, you have to do this". We both understand that we have aspirations. We work together to make it work. This is not the same for many young women. You hear women say, "I don't think my husband would let

me work in tech, it's too time consuming. I think I'll just have children and stay at home." They do that because they don't get the kind of support that they need. I believe you can do both: you can have children, bring them up and still live a life you consider meaningful. You don't have to lose yourself because you are trying to raise a family. I believe it's possible.'
Bolanle, 28

'Religion is very important to most Nigerians. It offers a form of escape. The downside is that people are complacent, they give up on this life because of hope for the next. But the upside is that it is a hopeful ideology to build their lives around. For me religion has helped me form ideals. I read a lot around other religions too, to help me form an overall world view. And it's a way to understand, relate and connect with people, too.' John, 34

'Nigerians are very religious, especially my parents' generation. The colonialists came with religion for us, and we dove in, as if we are the number one when it comes to religion. There is this high sense of morality, sanctimony, but at the end of the day they are still contributing to the problems that we have, and they won't let members of the LGBTQ+ community live their lives.' Osinachi, 30

'At times it feels that you are all alone. You're the only person who's queer, the only person who has all of these questions inside of you. There's not a lot you can say to people. You either have people of traditional African religions or Christianity or Islam, and that doesn't provide a lot of wriggle room.' S. I., 25

***

Waiting for an Uber on a busy street in Ikeja, the sound of praying and singing rises above the noise of the traffic. Behind a market stall and between two buildings – one of which houses a strip joint, the other a two-storey apartment – an open-sided marquee has been erected. Folding chairs are set out in rows, socially distanced, facing a huge TV screen on which a Pentecostal pastor is giving a rousing sermon. A dozen or more people of all ages – some men, most women – are spread throughout the tent. Some are standing, swaying, clapping their hands. Others are sitting, saying loud amens in time with the pastor. They are enraptured and engaged, oblivious to the sounds of traffic and the street life surrounding them.

Religion plays a significant role in Nigerian culture. With a population of 90 million Muslims, it is the fifth largest Muslim country in the world. Its more than 86 million Christians make it the sixth largest Christian country globally.[1] In Lagos, a primarily Christian city, churches proliferate. They range from historic buildings cast in the European mould or vast modern edifices resembling conference centres and designed to hold a congregation of thousands to smaller makeshift churches, like the street-side marquee. (Even the small Danfo buses that rule the streets of Lagos are stencilled with bible sayings – 'God is my shepherd', 'In God I trust' – and the more prosaic endorsement of the work ethic: 'Money no dey fall from heaven'.)

Religion is an area where some of the Soro Soke generation are beginning to find themselves conflicted. Most young Nigerians remain deeply religious. They often mention God in conversation. They speak of their relationship with God, their church, their pastor and the community of their congregation. They talk of how religion informs their family lives and their decisions and of the importance of prayer. They wake early on Sunday to attend a service; they tithe a portion of their income to the church. They bless each other and their families when they say goodbye.

'Nigeria is a very religious society; you are either Christian or Muslim and it's embedded in the foundation of everything. Family structure is very religious, we all go to church', says 30-year-old academic Priscilla Eke. 'I was born and raised Catholic and my parents are still practising Catholics but I choose to go to a Pentecostal church now. My parents understand – so long as I have a relationship with God, that's the most important thing. I go to a Pentecostal church because I love the way they worship, the vibe, the way they follow the scripture. I love to worship and the atmosphere there just suits my spirit. It doesn't mean I discard the process of Catholic Church in any way. I just feel that this is where I grow more in terms of my relationship with God.'

Osinachi, 30, is an artist who grew up in Aba, not far from Port Harcourt, in the south-east of Nigeria. He was exposed to two religions in childhood. 'My mum grew up in a very strict Catholic home, her elder sister is a reverend sister in the Catholic Church. I spent most of my time as a child with my aunt and at one point I aspired to being a reverend father. My dad came from a strong Jehovah Witness home. And it was by going to Kingdom Hall as a child that I learned to read Igbo fluently. They had these leaflets, Watchtower and Awake, that they translated, and they had really good translators, so it was well written in the Igbo language and you could read it and understand and enjoy.'

Nigeria is not alone in its religiosity. In their paper 'Religion and Social Transformation in Africa',[2] Obaji Agbiji and Ignatius Swart note that in many African countries, people who do not subscribe to any form of religion make up less than 0.1 per cent of the population. The pair find that religion 'constitutes an inextricable part of African society'. 'In the African worldview religion permeates the political and socio-economic life of Africans, just as politics, economic activities and other vital components of life permeate religion', they write.

According to Agbiji and Swart, political and economic elites across Africa often use religion to legitimise their power, and religious leaders have done little to confront that power in a bid to stem poverty and corruption.[3] Instead, in Nigeria, and elsewhere, religion has been used by politicians, political institutions, religious leaders and religious communities to foster and sustain the structural entrenchment of existing systems.[4]

This entrenchment is causing an internal struggle among some of the younger generation. They remain religious but find their aspirations and identity suppressed or denied by religious dictate. Young women can find the church policing their lives. Journalist Edwin Okolo, writing in *African Arguments* magazine, says religion in Nigeria 'is often elevated as fact and used to govern everything from reproductive rights to interpersonal relationships'.[5] Women, in particular, are held to high social mores. In some congregations, says Okolo, deacons scold female churchgoers for perceived slights to tradition, such as wearing their hair short.[6]

The younger cohort finds these conventions stifling and is beginning to challenge them. 'I grew up in a traditional Nigerian home, but I went to American and British schools and studied my Bachelor and Master's in the UK', says Eke. 'When I moved back to Lagos the culture just hit me and I couldn't get used to the way women are treated. Right from when I got there everyone was telling me how to behave and it made me very uncomfortable. Parents will tell you this part of the Bible says the way men or women should behave. But they pick or choose scriptures that support them and forget the rest. Religion is part of the weight that adds to the strong grip that men have on society, and they use religion and the Bible to hold on to this culture.'

In her paper 'Feminism Is the New Culture for Nigeria' Eke notes that Nigeria ranks 139 out of 156 countries in the world, and 32 out of 35 countries in sub-Saharan Africa, in terms of gender equality.[7] 'Within the Nigerian context, patriarchy is at the foundation of our culture and has established a belief system that supports and promotes the superiority of men over women', writes Eke.

A UN study in 2020 found that 28 per cent of 25- to 29-year-old Nigerian women have experienced some kind of violence since the age of 15, ranging from forced and early marriages to physical, mental or sexual assault.[8] And on an everyday level, the reach of patriarchal thought extends through society. Afrobarometer is a non-profit corporation that undertakes pan-African, non-partisan research on African experiences. In a survey of 1,599 Nigerian adults in January and February 2020, when asked the question 'who is the person who has primary responsibility for making decisions on behalf of your household?' only 14 per cent of female respondents, against 71 per cent of males, said they identified as the head of their household.[9] This imbalance is also reflected in the workplace.

'It's not equal in the work environment, certainly not', says Eke. 'Certain roles are pencilled in for only men to occupy – managing director, head of department, chairman, other leadership roles. You even hear women in the workplace tell you that you shouldn't aspire for those positions because it's not meant for you. In the mind of men and women there is a perception of the roles women should do. It doesn't matter your qualifications, your experience, you just cannot go further than a certain role.'

Young Nigerian women are increasingly pushing against these typical gender archetypes, says Ndeye Diagne, who oversaw the Africa Life survey at consultancy group Kantar. 'Equality is close to their heart', she says. 'There is a belief that gender stereotypes need to be addressed, that women should have the same opportunities. Stereotypes still exist of course but there is movement towards greater equality.'

Eke agrees. 'Younger women see things differently. Why are we working hard only to be stopped at a certain level?

How can we start cancelling out those ideas of this is a woman's job and this is not a woman's job? Some young women no longer have that mindset, that narrative that puts them on a certain level. They were brought up to dream and think big and go out and achieve. They had parents who did not think in terms of gender, instead raising their children based on interests. Their fathers pushed them and gave them the best education and encourage them to achieve. They are pushing at the glass ceiling and it's that positivity that gives me hope.'

Figure 18 Odunayo Eweniyi, 28, the co-founder and CEO of online savings and investment brand PiggyVest
Credit: Odunayo Eweniyi

Odunayo Eweniyi, 28, the co-founder and CEO of online savings and investment brand PiggyVest, is an example of the growing power of younger women in the workforce. As a keen defender of equal rights, Eweniyi's company has a diverse workforce. 'We went on a company retreat, and we released a team photo on social media. My team has slightly over 50 per cent representation of women. It was so strange for people to see more women than men that everyone started asking "is this an all women team?" It was a very interesting reaction to see', she says.

Working in the heavily male-dominated tech sector, Eweniyi has become used to fighting for her right to be heard as a woman – her Twitter account is ironically named 10X Tech Bro. She has found that success has given her a measure of equality that can elude other women. 'As I've gotten more successful, the way people treat me gets better. All of a sudden no one is asking questions as to why I am in the room. A decent amount of people know my name and the accompanying respect is not something they would accord a woman who has just started', she says.

In July 2020 she and a friend co-founded the Feminist Coalition with a mission to champion equality for women across society. 'We crystallised our needs into three pillars: women's health and safety, financial literacy, and legislative power for women', says Eweniyi. 'Everything I've read and a lot of my own views that I've imbibed from working is this: the difference between men and women, and the difference in their treatment, is a game of money and power. A very key part of the Feminist Coalition mission is helping women understand that money means power and that power is important.'

Along with gender inequality, homophobia is an issue that blights many young lives in Nigeria and across the continent. Many churches reinforce the idea that sexual minorities are an aberration caused by trauma or supernatural interference.[10] The Nigerian government's criminalisation of same-sex relations in the 2014 Same-Sex Marriage Prohibition Act was largely seen as an attempt by the then president, Goodluck Jonathan, to woo religious voters. The act not only penalises a same-sex marriage or civil union with 14 years imprisonment but also criminalises direct and indirect public display of, or support for, 'same sex relationships, gay clubs, societies, and organizations, processions, or meetings' with 10 years' imprisonment.[11]

This draconian legislation largely reflects wider public opinion. In the 2020 Afrobarometer research, Nigerians were very open to having neighbours of other ethnicities or religions but 89 per cent said they would strongly or somewhat dislike living next door to homosexuals.[12] And according to a report in the *Greenwich Social Work Review*, since the act was passed, violence against LGBTQ+ Nigerians has risen by 214 per cent.[13] 'Survivors frequently report arbitrary arrest and unlawful detention, invasion of privacy, physical assault and battery, and blackmail/extortion', says the report.[14]

Diagne agrees that LGBTQ+ rights are still largely a taboo subject. 'Religion makes it difficult. LGBTQ+ agendas are driven more from a diaspora perspective though some younger people, particularly those under 25, are more receptive to the idea, so it's not black and white', she says.

Journalist S. I. Ohumu, 25, identifies as queer. 'Acceptance is about a number of things. Age plays a part yes, but also the environment you grew up in, something as simple as the number of books you have read in your life', she says. 'I find people as young as myself or even younger still being very conservative, very close-minded. And you can't always fault them for that. The LGBTQ+ struggle for the most part is a question of privilege. If you grow up in a street where getting one meal a day is a struggle, I don't know that the foremost thing on your mind is being accepted for being gay.'

Artist Osinachi also identifies as queer and agrees that wealth is important. 'In Nigeria, what might protect you is your money', he says. 'In the sense that you get to live in an exclusive neighbourhood and on the road you are in your vehicle and nobody sees you. If you are effeminate, you just go from your vehicle into your house and go to special events and can afford to travel out of the country for a vacation and not really engage. But for the ones who don't have this luxury it is quite difficult. We hear stories about people being mobbed, families rejecting their own. We have lost a lot of human resources – I know a number of gay people who aspire to leave the country because they want to live freely. I can't hold a guy's hand, eyes would be on us; there are so many things that you can't do.'

Along with rising wealth, the diversity, anonymity and increasingly cosmopolitan nature of megacities like Lagos play a part in breaking down prejudices. In Lagos, the fashion industry's role in subverting gender norms has made it an ally to the queer community, leading some to call Lagos Fashion Week the unofficial Pride of Nigeria.[15] Brands such as unisex fashion label Bloke and androgynous menswear brand Orange Culture push the boundaries of traditional gender norms. The Orange Culture menswear collections feature bright colours and traditionally feminine elements such as crop tops, pussy bows and sequins. In interviews, founder Adebayo Oke-Lawal has said: 'For me, fashion continues to be an important way to investigate social dynamics.'[16]

Despite the criminalisation of homosexuality, speaking out is still a given for this generation. Osinachi is challenging sexual norms in his work. 'I think the first work I made confronting that subject was *Nduka's Wedding Day*', he says. The piece features a male figure in a wedding dress holding a bouquet. Another piece, *Becoming Sochukwuma*, depicts a male dancer pirouetting in a tutu and was inspired by 'I Will Call Him Sochukwuma: Nigeria's Anti-Gay Problem', an essay written by Chimamanda Adichie in reaction to the 2014 bill. Osinachi says his interpretation 'imagines Sochukwuma as a Nigerian queer man who grows up to love himself to the point of showing off his potential through dance'.

Writers and independent film-makers are also starting to give voice to LGBTQ+ stories. 'Nigeria is deeply homophobic and so is the film industry here', says screenwriter and director Uyaiedu Ikpe-Etim, 32. 'Nollywood is safe, commercial, conservative and homophobic. LGBTQ+ characters are seen as needing deliverance and even

Figure 19 *Becoming Sochukwuma* by Osinachi
Credit: Osinachi

subjects such as African traditional religions, voodoo for example, are demonised. When I started writing screenplays, I found I couldn't write the stories I wanted to write. I might write in a gay character here or there but often they didn't take it.'

When Ikpe-Etim released *Ìfé*, her directorial debut, in 2020, she faced the issue head on. *Ìfé* means love in the Yoruba language and the film is a lesbian love story. 'It's corny and soft and lovey-dovey and set over a three-day first date, which is kind of a thing in the lesbian community. People joke that when a lesbian says she's going on a date you can expect to see her in a week's time. We fall in love easily. I'm big on lesbian stereotypes, because why not?', says Ikpe-Etim.

The film was released online, to circumvent Nigeria's censorship laws, which currently only apply to films shown in cinemas. Even so, Alhaji Adebayo Thomas, the head of the country's censorship board NFVCB, put out a statement saying that Ipke-Etim could face 14 years in prison for 'promoting homosexuality on a screen'. 'There's a standing law that prohibits homosexuality, either in practice or in a movie or even in a theatre or on stage', he said.[17]

'Technically we didn't break any laws with the film, but the authorities are angry that we didn't give them a chance to censor it', says Ikpe-Etim. 'Politics is not yet dominated by young people and the people in authority now, all they know is how to bully and shut you down. They even sent letters to radio stations saying that broadcasters couldn't talk about the film on air.'

She believes the censorship board is out of touch with the way younger viewers feel. 'I think it's a great time for *Ìfé*. Everyone in the queer community is so excited about it and ready for it. We want to see queer people on TV, living normal lives. This film is not about struggle or homophobia – it's a story about two women in love.'

And, she says, Ìfé is at the forefront of a wave of queer-friendly work emerging from the Sore Soke generation. 'Gen Z have been born in a different time; they are not depending on one source for information – they have the Internet, not just church, school or family. And a lot of queer creatives are springing up, it's such an artistic community. In a few years from now there will be a lot of queer stories being told whether people are ready or not.'

In the Canvas8 2020 report 'Why Young Nigerians Are Rebelling against Tradition',[18] Caleb Somtochukwu Okereke, the managing editor of the digital publication *Minority Africa*, agrees there are clear generational differences. He suggests the online space is key to opening minds. 'There's a difference in how Gen Z Nigerians deal with LGBTQ+ issues and how Gen Y handles it', he writes. 'Gen Z Nigerians, in general, are more open to having dialogues about these issues than their Gen Y and Boomer counterparts, and while they are still homophobic, there's a noticeable difference in how they react and view these issues. Gen Z have access to the internet and information goes a [long] way in defining how they react to things like gender and sexuality.'[19]

Social media is altering this generation's social connections, which historically have been based on kinship and shared ethnic origins, but not everyone is happy with its progressive direction. Traditional values still carry weight with many young people. Davies Okeowo, 30, typifies the concerns about the impact social media is having in driving wider social change: 'I work a lot with young people between 17 and 24 years old and I think their priorities are misplaced. Hard work, respect, tolerance, the basic principles that make up our society, are being lost. There's a sense that you can become famous if you do something stupid on social media, and if you do it consistently you can make money doing it. Or they'll trade crypto, make a fast trade then cash out. There's a perception that "we can get it quick". I'm conservative and I believe advancement is made up of pillars and some are more important than others. Social media and technology will leave us better off economically but it's going to leave us worse off values wise.'

But there is no putting this genie back in the bottle: social media has created a space for more open dialogue, and minority groups are making their voices heard. Ipke-Etim is open about her sexuality on social media: she recently documented the experience of coming out to her mum on Twitter. 'Right now, queer people in Nigeria have become more visible and louder', she says. 'We use social media a lot. I'm on social media, I post about how I feel. I manage to be a very visible lesbian, to live my live loudly. It is somehow revolutionary. It shouldn't be but it is – I'm taking up space in a place where people don't want me to.'

As a public figure with a large social media following, Ohumu also uses her voice to raise LGBTQ+ issues online. 'Because being queer is criminalised in Nigeria, people are harassed by the police. It's serious. It's heavy. But it's also knowing that if you don't say anything, it won't change. If you are privileged enough, by virtue of your voice or your following or whatever that makes you not as vulnerable, then I think you have a responsibility to be open about it', she says. 'It's tricky to be open in the sense that you want to show that what you are doing is not wrong, but you are also concerned about what the law says. Twitter is one space where LGBTQ+ Nigerians are really voicing out and living their lives openly and having conversations. It's a safe place to have that conversation. From time to time you see LGBTQ+ trending on Nigerian Twitter, which is a very good thing. Although most of the comments you get are negative, the fact that the conversation keeps happening means people's minds are being changed.'

SPEAKING OUT: UYAIEDU IPKE-ETIM ON FACING HOMOPHOBIA

'Really bad things can happen simply because I'm a lesbian. People sometimes say "14 years" to me, to remind me that I am a criminal.'

Figure 20 Uyaiedu Ikpe-Etim, 32, is a film director and screenwriter who creates works that tell the stories of Nigeria's marginalised LGBTQ+ communities
Credit: Fati Abubakar

***

'Writing a film like Ìfé was seen as such a rebellious thing to do that people now see me as an activist but I actually feel that my whole life is a kind of activism. It's difficult being a lesbian in Nigeria but on most days that's not my only identity. It's the intersection of my identities that I have to navigate, because the majority of my identities are discriminated against. I am a woman, I am unmarried, I'm creative, I have tattoos and dreads and I'm a lesbian.

Really bad things can happen simply because I'm a lesbian. People sometimes say "14 years" to me, to remind me that I am a criminal. I just want to live a normal life. I want to love, I want to go out, hold hands, kiss, take pictures of my girlfriend and I together. But I don't have that. I sometimes say to my girlfriend "I want to love you in another country; I want our lives and our stories to be normal."

I don't have strong hope for the country. I'm pessimistic about Nigeria's future. There is a misogynistic, patriarchal culture and deeply ingrained homophobia. It's not just a problem with leadership. We, the people, are also problematic and oppressive. The average Nigerian has a very disturbing way to think about women and queer people. I'm conscious of the privilege I have, that I can go to places that are cosmopolitan and safe. This is not the story of the average lesbian in Nigeria. They don't have the means. Those kinds of places are expensive, and most people can't afford to visit them and there are a lot of places that are not safe for queer people.

In future, I hope to tell more queer stories, stories peppered and salted with queer characters. I want to get married and have a baby. I don't know if I can do that here. The thing is, I am so in touch with my Nigerian-ness and I want to raise my children to be in touch with theirs too. I don't want to have to raise them in the West just because it is illegal here. It reminds me of those lines from the Ijeoma Umebinyuo poem: too foreign for home / too foreign for here. / never enough for both.'

SPEAKING OUT: MICHAEL ELÉGBÈDÉ ON THE DIASPORA

'We need to create dialogues between Africans and African Americans and Black people globally, because the success of Africa is the success of Black people everywhere.'

***

'I was born here. I grew up with my grandmother and went to primary school here and I had a lot of resonance with Nigerian culture. But in 2002, when I was 12 going on 13, I moved to America

Figure 21 Michael Elégbèdé, 32, is chef and founder of Lagos fine dining restaurant Ítàn Test Kitchen
Credit: Fati Abubakar

to be with my parents. My mum had a restaurant in Chicago – it was Nigerian food, well specifically Yoruba food. I worked at the restaurant when I went to grade school and after university I got to a point where I realised that being a chef is what I want to do. So I went to culinary school in Napa Valley, worked around California and then went to New York to work at 11 Madison Park.

Throughout this whole experience I found myself in a place of almost losing my drive, my aspiration, everything I loved about food, because of the realities that surrounded my experiences in these white-dominated, Euro-centric, highly racist cultures. You look at the history of Black people in these types of restaurants, they've been operating for over 10 years and there hasn't been any Black sous chef. Not that there hasn't been any Black staff. You would have someone who comes in from Scandinavia, spends two months then gets promoted. I'm working just as hard as any of them, I'm just as good as any of them but I would have comments like "yeah you're good but you're probably going to end up frying chicken somewhere". Everything that surrounded that reality started making me lose myself and lose my desire to be in food.

I saw myself going down a very bad rabbit hole and I started asking myself what made me fall in love with cooking in the first place. And the answer was our food, my food. Cooking Euro-centric food day in and day out wasn't telling my story. I didn't see myself in what I was doing and that's what it should be about. So, I bought a one-way ticket and moved back home. I started travelling around the country, cooking in remote areas, diverse areas, learning and literally falling in love with Nigeria in a way that very few people get to do.

Black food culture, what we do here, is often overlooked. We've done a representation of northern Nigerian food, a menu from the south-east, from the south-west, and a menu about the diaspora. I've never seen African Americans as different to us but developing the diaspora menu brought me so much closer, in a way that I didn't expect. I had to think of what it would feel like as a Nigerian who loves Nigeria and loves my culture, to be taken to a place of nothingness and trying to find something to grab onto that is home. I was so heartbroken, in a way that I've never been. I've been heartbroken over slavery and being in racist environments, but I've never really put myself in a position to feel the pain of being taken away. That was a very painful place to go to. And then it became lighter the more I found dishes that evolved from West African food into something just as beautiful. And that was what this menu was to me: an exploration of our stories, our narratives and really understanding what it felt like to have gone through that.

It is very important for Africans and African Americans to create platforms that exchange narratives, that allow us to find synergies in our stories, in our realities, in our cultures. To find those bridges. They are there, we just need to go back and trace them. Black people in America standing up for their rights is giving the appetite to other movements like #endSARS here. There's this cross-pollination that's always there but we are not aware, or at least not bringing it to light. We need to create dialogues between Africans and African Americans and Black people globally, because the success of Africa is the success of Black people everywhere. The expression of Africa in its truest form, in a genuine form, is a pride for all Black people. At the core of it for everyone in general but especially for Black people.'

5 JAPÁ

'When people make some money or have some opportunity, often they don't want to raise their children in Nigeria. When we reach a certain level of financial independence, most of us want to leave for better pay, better security, better standards of living. Most people are not looking to become millionaires – they just want a greater degree of certainty and security about the future, better healthcare, things like that.'
John, 34

'I am trying to emigrate to Australia. I went to university, I'm trained as an engineer, but I'm working as a waiter because there are no jobs. I'm married now and it is hard to raise a family on what I'm earning. In Australia they are looking for people with my qualifications and they have jobs for us. It's a long way away but I would like to go. At least for a few years.'
Abiodun, 28

'I want to go to Canada. As long as you have a degree, a skill that is well needed, like software developers, you can go. I want to live somewhere else, and just come back to visit.'
Uzor, 28

'Young Nigerians are living in terror and a lot of activists are leaving the country. It's not safe, people like DJ Switch, who is at the height of her career, are leaving. Many of the brightest minds are leaving.' Rinu, 23

'It feels like every week one of my acquaintances is moving to another country. My friends think I'm crazy because I still work for a Nigerian employer. The currency is shit and I have *the skills to work for other people who would pay me in dollars or pounds. With a bit of effort, I can leave this country if I wanted to. My ultimate dream in life is to have land in New Zealand, a small sustainable house in the middle of a forest, and just come back when I miss my family.'* S. I., 25

'*Many of those who have the opportunity to leave the country are going but I've never been one to believe in leaving. I'm in my fatherland and I feel like a king here. I love my country so much; I knew that no matter what, I was going to make it here, because there are a lot of opportunities in Nigeria.'* Osinachi, 30

***

Lagos offers many opportunities but life in a megacity is exhausting. For the very poor, it is a daily struggle to survive. Even for those with a measure of economic security, the failure of infrastructure, the long commutes, the constant hustle for success can wear thin. *Japá* is a Yoruba word that translates as 'run away'. The word has become part of this generation's lexicon, defining the desire of many young Nigerians to make, or at least experience, a new life abroad. Research suggests as many as 57 per cent would consider leaving the country to work or study abroad if it were possible, though less than 10 per cent are making actual preparations, such as getting a visa.[1]

Journalist S. I. Ohumu, 25, is one who is toying with the idea. 'I want to not live here for a bit. Nigeria is tedious right now. I don't know how it feels to have stable electricity – I know at any point in time my power is going to get cut. I don't know what it feels like for the state to provide water for me. I have to dig boreholes and fuck up my water table. I don't know what it feels like to have something like the NHS. If I get sick, I'm one health emergency away from bankruptcy', she says.

According to the International Organization for Migration (IOM), the majority of African emigrants look within the continent for opportunities: in 2019, over 21 million were living in another African country.[2] Intra-Africa migration is not always easy. South Africa remains the preferred destination, with around four million migrants living in the country.[3] But domestic political, economic and social crises in South Africa have led to the scapegoating of migrants by public officials, reinforcing existing xenophobic sentiments among the public.[4]

Magnum Muyiwa is 34. He now lives in Lagos, where he runs a chain of kiosks that offer electronic cash withdrawal, but he spent several years living in South Africa. 'I moved to South Africa and opened a small chain of barber shops there', he says. 'I was making a lot of money, but the South Africans don't like Nigerians. We work hard and we make money, and they think we are taking things away from them. There was a riot and they burned down all the Nigerian businesses. I lost my biggest shop, so I came home.'

Of those who look further afield for opportunities, a 2019 report found that almost 80 per cent are driven by the hope for better economic or social prospects and that most are young, educated and relatively wealthy: able to meet tough visa requirements and to afford the fees and costs of travelling and living abroad.[5]

Ohumu's ambitions are typical. 'I want a Master's in Journalism and I'm not going to study here', she says. 'I'm thinking of Goldsmiths – they have a very interesting digital journalism course – and I like Columbia and McGill in Canada, too. I'm focusing right now on getting scholarships.'

Influencer and entrepreneur John Obidi, 34, moved to Dubai to grow his career. 'I emigrated to the UAE eight months ago', he says. He had a choice of destinations. 'Canada has its doors wide open to talented Nigerians, so does the US. Countries like that can attract the best and the brightest and Nigeria becomes a farm for talent – Saudi Arabia has more Nigerian doctors than Nigeria has.'

The issue of brain drain is real. Nigeria sends the largest number of African students abroad – some 95,000 – and ranks fifth in the world in terms of the overall number of students in foreign study.[6] Some 374,000 Nigerians live in the US, making them the largest African migrant group according to the United States Census Bureau.[7] The *Financial Times* says Nigerians in the US are the most highly educated of all groups in the country, with 61 per cent holding at least a Bachelor's degree (compared with 31 per cent of the total foreign-born population and 32 per cent of the US-born population).[8] More than half of Nigerian immigrants were likely to occupy management positions, compared with 32 per cent of the total foreign-born population and 39 per cent of the US-born population.[9]

'Gifted young Nigerians have other viable options and most of the people who have the ability and drive to change the country emigrate', says Ohumu. She echoes widely held perceptions that much of the country's young people are looking to leave. Writing in *The Republic*, John Babalola, a public policy analyst in Lagos, says: 'For a lot of Nigerians, relocating abroad with little or no intent to return has become a life goal. For some, the Nigerian project requires abandonment.'[10] But, both within Africa and in the Global North, the number of African and Nigerian immigrants is vastly overestimated.

The share of Africans living abroad has barely increased since the 1960s.[11] According to the United Nations Department of Economic and Social Affairs (DESA), in 2017, of the 258 million international migrants worldwide, only 36 million were African, around 14 per cent of the total and equal to just under 3 per cent of Africa's population.[12] In 2019, according to the IOM, more than 40 per cent of all international migrants were born in Asia, primarily originating from India, China, Bangladesh, Pakistan and Afghanistan.[13] Mexico was the second largest country of origin, and the Russian Federation was fourth. Several European countries have sizable populations of emigrants, including Ukraine, Poland, the United Kingdom and Germany.[14] Of the top 20 countries of emigrants, not one was from mainland sub-Saharan Africa.[15]

DESA estimated Nigeria's diaspora at 1.7 million in June 2020,[16] less than 1 per cent of the country's population. But perhaps because it is the most talented that usually make their way abroad, this 1 per cent is a powerful and important interest group. Diaspora Nigerians continue to have a significant impact on their home nation, not least financially. For four consecutive years, official remittances from diaspora Nigerians have exceeded the country's oil revenues.[17] According to the Nigeria White Paper by consulting group PWC, the diaspora accounted for US$23.63 billion in remittances in 2018: an amount that is equal to 6.1 per cent of Nigeria's GDP and 80 per cent of the

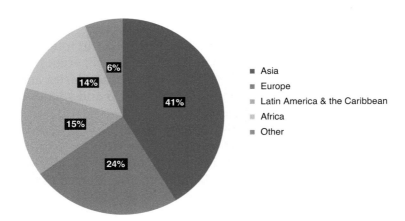

Figure 22 Percentage of total global migrants by their continent of origin
Source: www.un.org/development/desa/pd/content/international-migrant-stock

country's budget.[18] This amount is also 11 times the foreign direct investment flow into the country during the same period.

Young diaspora Nigerians also have a softer, though no less important, role to play as cultural ambassadors. Successful Nigerian musician Davido has had over a billion streams of his music online. Speaking to Trevor Noah on *The Daily Show*, he credited the Nigerian diaspora for its role in his success: 'With my music, it started from Atlanta, from Nigerians being in the club and telling the DJ, "I'm going to spend money today but play Davido's music when my bottles are coming out." Or females asking the DJ "play his song, play his song". In 2013, I sold out every venue, 20 shows across the US, without exposure so I have to give a shout out to the diaspora people that supported us.'[19]

Recognising the importance of the diaspora, the Nigerian federal government established the Nigerians in Diaspora Commission in 2017, to maximise the human, capital and material resources of this demographic and to try to engage diasporic Nigerians in national policies and projects. And many diaspora Nigerians remain heavily invested in Nigeria, emotionally and financially.

Oyindamola Shoola, 24, is studying in the US but also runs an online organisation promoting, supporting and developing young writers within Nigeria. 'When people ask, I say I'm Nigerian. I come from Nigeria. No matter how much I associate myself with another identity – I got American citizenship this year – my Nigerian-ness will always come through. It comes through in my accent, my name, my sarcasm. The perspective of things as a Nigerian is also different, and that Nigerian spirit is just inside me', she says. 'Home is different from here. There is a community, it allows you to have peace of mind, it's more relaxing, less demanding, more peaceful and there is more support. At the moment, I'm being exposed to different cultures and different things and it's hard for me to say I want to go to one place and settle there. But I want to go back when I know that my presence is meaningful, and I can do something tangible.'

Shoola highlights another aspect of migration that is often disregarded: a growing number of young African immigrants are choosing to leave the West and return home. In a project for *The African Perspective Magazine* and Deutsche Welle, film-maker Ras Mutabaruka created a series called *Homecoming in 2020*, which documented the return of eight young African women.[20] These included Navalayo Osembo, who resigned from her United Nations job in New York to move back to Kenya and start Enda, Africa's first running shoe company; and Nathalie Munyampenda, who gave up a job with the Canadian government and moved back to Rwanda to work with the Next Einstein Forum at the African Institute for Mathematical Sciences.

'In all of my time living and working in the West, I have yet to meet a young African professional who doesn't dream of one day moving back to the continent', writes Mutabaruka for Deutsche Welle.[21] 'Besides systemic barriers that prevent many from fully realizing their potential abroad, this generation doesn't just want to work for a pay check. They want to know that what they are doing is valuable and has a real impact on real people. They want to be a part of the continent's rebirth.'

Nigerian tech entrepreneur Iyinoluwa Aboyeji, 31, illustrates Mutabaruka's point. The growing opportunities that Lagos offers helped lure him back from the US and he has now launched Future Africa, an early-stage venture fund that connects African investors with local start-ups. 'We work very closely with local companies', he says. 'Without early-stage capital that gets someone past their first year, a lot of young entrepreneurs can't get off the ground. We connect them with local investors who have an affinity to the problems on the ground and make sure that we get them that early-stage money.'

But a sense of identity and belonging also played a part in his decision to return home. 'I feel more powerful in Africa than I do in the US or any other part of the world', he says. 'I don't have to contest my humanity here. I am a very different person in the US, where I have to contend, where I have to ask: Am I real?'

Immigration can offer young people a real opportunity, to learn new skills and make new connections. The true challenge lies not in preventing japá but in encouraging young people to utilise their period spent abroad to enrich themselves with skills and knowledge and, then, in building a country that is secure and with sufficient opportunity to attract them home again.

'We need a Nigeria where a common graduate can get a job that pays enough to save and to live', says 23-year-old Rinu Oduala. 'Where law enforcement doesn't abuse the rights of citizens. We need peace, dignity and justice so that young people can really breathe and where Nigerians living abroad can come home and feel safe.'

SPEAKING OUT: DAVIES OKEOWO ON ENTREPRENEURSHIP

'I know he's not always popular, but Donald Trump really made it happen for me. I saw The Apprentice *and I thought, "this is what I want to do with my life". To run a business, to employ people, to create opportunities.'*

***

'I grew up in not so good circumstances, in a polygamous home and didn't see my father a lot. Sometimes I would go years without seeing him even though he lived only 30 minutes away. We

Figure 23 Davies Okeowo, 30, is an entrepreneur and the winner of *Next Titan*, Nigeria's version of *The Apprentice*
Credit: Davies Okeowo

didn't live in a slum, but it was a low-income neighbourhood, and it wasn't very rosy. One of the choices my parents made that I'm grateful for was putting me in a very good private primary school. It was my first glimpse of what could be.

In high school, business studies and accounting were my favourite subjects. I love commerce. For me it's easy to understand and comprehend. I studied accounting at university – I was the first person in my family to go to university and get a degree.

In my second year I had a realisation of what entrepreneurship could be. I know he's not always popular, but Donald Trump really made it happen for me. I saw The Apprentice and I thought, "this is what I want to do with my life". To run a business, to employ people, to create opportunities. From that point on I was focusing on entrepreneurship. I watched DVDs, listened to audio recordings, attended seminars and read books by Richard Branson and people like that.

I've never taken a job, I've always been full-time in entrepreneurship. After university, in 2014, I started my first business, but it didn't work out. Then on the 31st of October of that year, I was stuck in a traffic jam with my mentor. What should have been a 25-minute journey took three hours and she helped me to really identify my skills and focus my efforts. So, for once Lagos traffic was helpful to me!

She told me that a common challenge for SMEs [small and medium enterprises] and micro businesses is that they need accountancy and financial advice but can't afford a full-time accountant. The following month, I met my co-founder and, in January 2015, Enterprise Hill was born. We were aiming to help small and micro businesses in Nigeria get more profitable, by building accounting and financial structures. The business grew organically until August 2015 and then I took part in Next Titan.

Next Titan is Nigeria's version of The Apprentice. When I won, my parents were jumping for joy and dancing. It was the first time in my life I really made my parents feel that way. It was very special. I won five million naira (around US$12,000), which gave *me the opportunity to take care of my family and also to invest in Enterprise Hill. That's when the real show started.*

Thanks to mentorship I was quite grounded and I didn't see the money as making it big; I saw it more as five million reasons why I can't fail.'

6 ENTREPRENEURS WITH A MISSION

'My first interaction with a mission-driven company was Andela, and it was there I fully understood what it means to serve people and change their lives, because I saw it happen every day: some middle-class kid or poor kid, turning their life around in an incredible way by us giving them the skills of software development and the opportunity to build a very viable global skill that would get them where they wanted to go.' Iyinoluwa, 31

'Education is important in Nigeria. My generation, those born in the 1990s, we know that if we want to make it, we have to be educated. The problem is that even people with a Master's degree have no connection to the real world. They don't know the difference between an invoice and a receipt. We launched Competence Africa in 2017. We offer courses across a blend of skills such as accounting technology and soft skills like teamwork and leadership. We also focus on tech-enabled skills that can really give people a hand up.' Davies, 30

'If you look at how we live in Nigeria, we don't have a credit system. Because there is no credit system, when you want to buy something, like a car, you are dropping the bulk sum. If you want to rent a house you are paying a year or two years in advance. If you want to go to school, you are paying up-front. And when you look at that system, young people were at a disadvantage. The idea for us was how about we give you a place where you are putting some money for a particular purpose: cars, houses, school. You can access it every 90 days, so we are forcing you to save in 90-day bursts and we are *paying you interest that is above inflation rate and we are not charging you.'* Odunayo, 28

'*There are so many needs here that it is easy to become a hero. You just have to step forward and address them. I founded Headstart Africa as a Facebook group to answer questions around business. Anyone could come and learn about business, personal development and how to succeed in Nigeria and Africa. Anyone could ask a question and I would try to answer or find someone who could.'* John, 34

***

Figure 24 Oyindamola Shoola, 24, leader of SpringNG, a 'literary movement' for Nigerian young writers
Credit: Oyindamola Shoola

Oyindamola Shoola is sitting in a high-backed black leather office chair that looks a bit like a modern-day throne. It's a fitting seat for a woman who, at just 24, is already a published writer, mentor to a host of other young writers and the founder and leader of SprinNG, an organisation that is beginning to build the foundations of a literary industry in Nigeria.

Shoola and her high school friend Kanyinsola Olorunnisola co-founded SprinNG in 2016, when they were still teenagers. The organisation bills itself as 'a literary movement for the promotion, revitalization, and improvement of new Nigerian generations in writing and literature'.[1] It promotes the biographies of 350 young writers and publishes their work on its website. SprinNG also runs a poetry prize, offers an annual women author's prize and a series of free writing fellowships, where aspiring writers are connected to mentors to help develop their work. There's a well-structured manual to support the process and other free resources, including learning materials and mobile phone minutes to enable mentees to connect with their mentors. More than 160 writers had been mentored by the end of 2021. To date the organisation has been self-funded. 'For the first five years SprinNG has been funded by our own money. We work as volunteers, we still have day jobs', says Shoola.

Despite the international success of Nigerian writers such as Chinua Achebe, Ben Okri and Chimamanda Ngozi Adichie, young writers in Nigeria lack both cultural and structural support. 'In Nigeria, there aren't the structural resources to help young people who have these awesome stories to tell', says Shoola. 'There is no Master's in Creative Writing programme for example, so if anyone wants to study they have to travel abroad. And most publishers in Nigeria are simply printers. They print the book and then hand it back to the author to distribute and sell. Literary agents are also usually abroad so most of our books are published overseas. An American wouldn't send their work to a Nigerian publisher for publication, so why don't we have the resources in Nigeria to host our voices and promote them? The audience for Nigerian books is mostly here in Nigeria but people struggle to access books; they are expensive because they are published abroad. It irks me. I want to start a book publishing company in Nigeria that provides full holistic support to writers and takes the audience of Nigerian readers very seriously, instead of just wanting to ship our authors' work outward.'

Shoola's vision, drive and wider social focus are not unusual in the Soro Soke generation. Nigeria is one of the world's most innovative nations: the *Harvard Business Review* highlights its 'powerful entrepreneurial climate', and points to the success of world-leading Nigerian businesses such as Jumia, Interswitch, Kobo360 and Andela, across sectors including education, fintech, agriculture, healthcare, logistics and travel.[2] And much of the country's entrepreneurial growth is being driven by its young people. The International Youth Foundation's 2017 Global Youth Index surveyed young people in 29 countries. It found that Nigeria ranks first in the world for commercial energy, with 40 per cent of young Nigerians engaged in early-stage entrepreneurial activity.[3]

'Money and success have been de-tabooed and 95 per cent of Gen Z across Africa aspire to financial success', says Ndeye Diagne, who heads up the Kantar Africa Life survey. 'Young people are also very confident in their ability to set up and materialise a business, especially in Nigeria, where more than 76 per cent of our 2019 respondents said they intend to set up a business. This compares to around 40 per cent for the same age in the US. Young people here are purpose driven, action oriented and very entrepreneurial.'

The beating heart of the country's entrepreneurial energy is in Lagos, where a hustle or side hustle are almost ubiquitous. In part this is driven by financial need – according to Nigeria's National Bureau of Statistics (NBS), youth unemployment and underemployment stood at 42.5 per cent in Q4 2020.[4] With jobs scarce and often badly paid, a business on the side helps make ends meet. But it's also a cultural attitude. Entrepreneurial nous flows through this generation's veins.

'In Lagos you sometimes get the feeling that your life is incomplete if you're not an entrepreneur or you don't at least have a side hustle or two', says Tamara Ojeaga, 39, who knows of what she speaks – alongside her day job in marketing, she runs a sportswear business on the side.

'My activewear line is called Rude Activewear', says Ojeaga. 'We want to be the Nike or lululemon for Africa. We use our knowledge of local wants and needs to fill gaps. We consider local sizing – we have thicker thighs and bottoms – and we know that people here want to look cool and sexy even when we are working out. In our first collection we infused Ankara patterns into the designs to offer something we can relate to.'

Ojeaga's business highlights a growing trend – entrepreneurship focused on local and pan-African consumers. A growing proportion of Nigeria's large youth population has money to spend and are seeking out products that cater to their tastes. The pan-African market, long hindered by red tape and lack of infrastructure, just got more accessible, too. On 1 January 2021, the 54 African countries opened their markets to each other and duty-free trading of goods and services across borders began. The new market, created under the African Continental Free Trade Area agreement, is estimated to be as large as 1.3 billion people, with a combined GDP of US$3.4 trillion, making it the largest free trade area in the world.[5]

Ojeaga's business is hosted on Instagram, reflecting another trend: young entrepreneurs are using virtual spaces, in particular social media, as a business tool. Diagne says: 'Social commerce has really taken off in Nigeria.

Entrepreneurship for this generation is fuelled by social media. Instagram is basically a place to sell. WhatsApp and Facebook, too. Gen Z in particular use these tools to sell physical products and services.'

John Obidi, 34, is a Nigerian influencer and entrepreneur and his business-focused Facebook group has 167,000 followers across Africa. 'Social media is a way to reach a really large audience', he says. 'Females in Nigeria is a group that has more than one million members, all women, discussing issues relevant to females. YouTube is another important outlet. A friend of mine launched Money Africa, teaching people how to save and invest and she now has 100,000 followers.'

But being a young entrepreneur on the continent still poses significant challenges. As with anywhere in the world, starting a business requires a willingness to hustle and hustle some more. It requires entrepreneurial skills, ambition and a lot of hard work. In Nigeria, especially, starting a business is not easy. Funding is hard to secure, infrastructure is unreliable and government regulations are not supportive: in its inaugural African Tech Ecosystems of the Future report in 2021, FDI, a specialist division of the *Financial Times*, found that Nigeria had the highest volume of start-ups on the African continent, over 750, but that it missed out on all the top 10 rankings for categories that are critical to helping a business thrive.[6] And alongside the usual challenges there are some that are particular to the region.

Odunayo Eweniyi, who co-founded and heads up financial services brand PiggyVest, says: 'Nigeria is an emerging economy; Africa is an emerging economy. That means businesses face unique challenges, like the non-existence of credit infrastructure. Or non-existence of several kinds of infrastructure. The regulatory environment is very unstable and there are security problems. As a founder, you need to build your team and find an office, but you also need to generate your own power because power is not reliable, and you are responsible for security because security is iffy as well. It's like running a mini country. We are responsible for things that a founder in the US doesn't have to think about.'

These issues cut across sectors. Chef Michael Elégbèdé, 32, opened Ítàn Test Kitchen, a fine dining restaurant in Lagos, in 2017. 'Chefs and critics outside Nigeria don't understand the realities that we have to overcome', he says. 'I have to be the one to supply my water, my electricity. To make sure staff are safe, we have lodging for them. In most other parts of the world, there are culinary schools. I don't have that luxury; we don't have a culinary school that is of standard. For the level of excellence that I want to provide, I literally do a paid training of every member of staff because I also understand that we are not in a reality where I can have people come and train for free. They can't afford to. I'm fine with it, I like the fact that I am able to do this here and to do it in a way that is good, but these are the realities that we face compared to other places, especially if you want to do it in a way that shows humanity.'

Acting with humanity is a growing consideration – the typical Soro Soke generation entrepreneur is a creative disruptor, using their business to deliver solutions to the larger problems the continent faces. As Adesuwa Omorede and Sara Thorgren point out in their paper 'Passionate Leaders in Social Entrepreneurship: Exploring an African Context', non-state actors are increasingly influential in addressing pressing social needs in sub-Saharan Africa, across everything from health to illiteracy, agriculture and finance.[7] These social enterprises are not only solving problems. A Siemens Stiftung analysis of 12 African countries estimates that by 2030, one million new jobs can be created by local social enterprises.[8]

For Elégbèdé, showing humanity goes beyond his immediate staff. When he struggled to find produce and supplies at the quality he needs, he set up a foundation to incentivise, train and support his rural suppliers: 'We work with people in the perceived lower tier of society to help them bring up their businesses', he says. 'For example, all the plates we use in the restaurant are made by local women living in villages. Their traditional plates are regular thick, clay plates and we asked them to make refined version for us. It takes more work for them but there's also a lot more money in it. Because we are asking for a certain value and certain quality, we are willing to pay for it. What we are doing is creating avenues that educate people to be able to stand on their own two feet.'

Omobolanle Banwo, 28, runs her own design agency, Geneza Brands, and a training business, the Geneza School of Design, which offers online courses for students in 14 countries across Africa. In 2018 she noticed a dearth of women in the Nigerian design industry and launched the Female Designer Movement, which offers a free training programme for women who want to build a career in design.

Figure 25 Omobolanle Banwo, 28, founder of the Female Designer Movement
Credit: Fati Abubakar

'I asked myself why we don't have more women designers and I did a bit of research and realised that women have this preconceived notion that design is just for men. I wanted to change that narrative. In 2018, I put out a post saying I would train women for free. In my mind I was expecting about 10 or 15 women to take up the opportunity but almost 300 women applied. So, we ran another course and another and we just kept on training women, training women. So far, I've trained over 3,000 women for free', she says.

'We take a percentage of what we earn from our online school to sponsor women in the Female Designer Movement. In this way we have a sustainable system and we don't have to rely on other organisations for money or sponsorship. I'm really happy that we have all these systems in place to prove that we are serious about what we are doing because it's not just about having a passion, it's also about creating structure around it and being accountable', says Banwo.

She sums up the way many young entrepreneurs think when she says: 'My values are about empowering people. I'm the kind of person who likes to create opportunities for others. I don't like to win alone. I want other people to win with me.'

Banwo has the ambition to offer her free training programme to women outside Nigeria, too. 'I have a goal and desire to train many African women and we are currently trying to collaborate with other African countries', she says. And she points to technology as the great enabling factor. Whether it is her design business or her pan-African training offer, it is access to the Internet that is facilitating her success. 'With Geneza Brands we've worked with more international organisations than Nigerian organisations', she says. 'They want to give a global brand an African feel, so they reach out to us. I've had the opportunity to work with established organisations in Gabon, the UK and the US on different branding projects.'

'When I check my email in the morning, I'm receiving emails from people asking me to do what I love to do and offering me a lot of money to do it', says Banwo. 'This is the life! I wish I could express what I feel on the inside. Imagine: I am able to train women all over Africa, all over Nigeria, from my computer, right here in my house. Imagine such an opportunity!'

7 THE NEW OIL

'This is not being dramatic, this is not an exaggeration – for young Nigerians and young Africans, technology is literally freedom. In Nigeria, the path to money usually lies in politics, oil and gas or telecommunications, and those sectors are notoriously hard to break into. Before the tech space arrived in Nigeria, if you talked about getting a job you would hear people say that you have to have connections. That's basically our term for nepotism: you have to know someone to get a job in those sectors. But in tech there is a very real meritocracy at work. You are only limited by your own skills and that is really something for us. This is a path that no one else controls.'
Odunayo, 28

'Technology is a great equaliser. In my parents' time, you were stuck with the hand you were dealt. You were dealt Nigeria, and Nigeria was all you had. My generation has technological tools that can get us out. We can go online and work for overseas clients. There are business and income opportunities with clients who are in Dubai, Spain, the US or the UK. We can be paid for our skills in dollars and that creates an alternate reality. We have better purchasing power, we can bridge the gap, we can access more than the hand we were dealt. It's a huge opportunity.' Davies, 30

'From the point of view of a digital artist, I don't need to pay rent for a studio, my studio is basically my laptop, and I can just wake up and start working at my desk. I also don't need to worry about buying and priming a canvas and all that. But starting out in digital art I never really thought about

all that. My dad introduced me to the Internet. When the Internet came, in the early 2000s, he took me to a cybercafé one Saturday. It was far from home, and we walked there together. I sat with him, he opened the computer and created my first email account, showed me how to visit websites and send emails. After that, whenever I had money – it cost 100 naira for one hour, which was a lot back then – I would go to buy an hour, browse the Internet. I started creating abstract works using Word. Those were my early works and I've gone on from there. Now, I'm showing my work at art fairs around the world. In 2021, I headlined an African art fair in London and my work was auctioned at Christie's, the first time they auctioned a [digital work] by an African. I'm super excited to be leading the way for Africa, so Africans can see what is possible. Because this is what is possible – a digital artwork made by an African can sell for US$70,000 and higher.'
Osinachi, 30

***

Technology has changed our world. Though we may complain about the overarching influence of the Internet and mobile telephony on our daily lives, they are also vehicles for connection, freedom of expression and freedom of opportunity. Arguably, nowhere has their influence been more powerfully felt than in sub-Saharan Africa, where there has been an extraordinary technological takeup, particularly by this young cohort.

Even the oldest members of the Soro Soke generation had very limited access to internet technology – as recently as a decade ago, fewer than 5 per cent of sub-Saharan Africans had access to the Internet.[1] Today, internet penetration varies widely but as of December 2020, approximately 85 per cent of Kenyans and 73 per cent of Nigerians had internet access.[2]

Access is improving each year – in October 2021, tech behemoth Google announced plans to invest US$1 billion

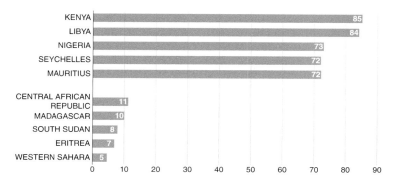

Figure 26 African countries with highest and lowest percentage of population with internet access
Source: www.statista.com/statistics/1124283/internet-penetration-in-africa-by-country

in Africa over the next five years to deliver better access to fast and cheaper Internet.[3] This growing connectivity is empowering a generation with opportunities that would have been unthinkable as little as 10 years ago. The World Bank's International Finance Corporation predicts that by 2025, the internet economy has the potential to contribute US\$180 billion to Africa's economy, growing to US\$712 billion by 2050. Increasing internet penetration across the continent to 75 per cent has the potential to create 44 million new jobs, it says.[4] Even governments are beginning to recognise the potential of technology. In June 2021, when the Lagos state government announced its intention to construct West Africa's biggest technology cluster, Lagos state governor Babajide Sanwo-Olu described technology as 'the new oil', highlighting its potential to generate wealth and jobs for its young population.[5]

Tech talent in Africa is at a historical peak and continues to rise annually. There are 690,000 professional developers across Africa[6] and the continent has seen an extraordinary growth of tech hubs, too, most championed by young people – places where tech talent, innovative thinkers and entrepreneurs come together to create new digital products and businesses.[7] Google recently launched its Africa Investment Fund, through which it will invest US$50 million in local start-ups and provide them with access to its employees, network and technologies.[8] Technology enables this skilled young workforce to compete for jobs and projects abroad on a more equal footing and to earn higher wages in foreign currencies.

In a country and continent where youth unemployment is a major issue, the tech sector not only offers this cohort access to well-paid jobs but also the possibility to build an industry based on meritocracy. In the past, bright young Nigerians would vie for jobs in the public sector or oil and gas industry, fields that are rampant with nepotism. To be able to build successful businesses and find jobs, independent of corruption, is liberating, both for individuals and for society.

Odunayo Eweniyi, 28, who co-founded PiggyVest, now employs 70 staff. 'The youth unemployment rate is very high. I graduated from university with a first-class degree in engineering, but I was faced with the very real possibility of not getting a job', she says. 'Being able to work in tech, I created a job for myself and we've gone on to create jobs for other people, running into the hundreds. And that's not possible anywhere else, only in tech. Your limit in tech is your imagination, you are the only one in your own way, which is amazing. You can't say that for literally any other sector here. Every day when we take stock of the work we've done and the team we've built, the path the company has charted and everyone else who has come up with their own company as a result of PiggyVest, it is all a joy. Because that's many people who've moved from unemployment to working.'

PiggyVest is an online savings and investment platform that is largely accessed by mobile phone and it is the mobile telecoms revolution that arguably has had the largest impact in sub-Saharan Africa. According to research conducted in 2020 by the Berlin Institute for Population and Development, in the year 2000 just 550,000 out of 122 million Nigerians had fixed-line phone connections.[9] Connections were not expected to grow significantly: the technical challenge of installing infrastructure was simply too great and the costs unlikely to be recouped. Then, in 2001, South African company MSN installed a much cheaper mobile network. Almost overnight, mobile telephony became a mass phenomenon – by 2004, there were nine million subscribers in the country; by 2019, 185 million Nigerians had a mobile contract.[10]

This is a statistic that is repeated across the region. As early as 2016, *The Economist* found that mobile phone ownership in sub-Saharan Africa (then at 40 per cent) was more widespread than access to electricity.[11] By 2020, there were 930 million SIM connections in the region, representing 77 per cent of the population.[12]

The use of smartphones, which enable greater access to mobile technology, is also growing. In Nigeria, one of the countries with the largest number of mobile internet

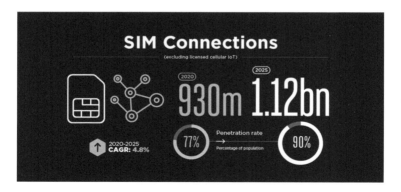

Figure 27 Predicted growth in Sub-Saharan African SIM connections, 2020–2025

Source: www.gsma.com/mobileeconomy/sub-saharan-africa/

users worldwide, some 75 per cent of web traffic is generated via smartphones.[13] Nigeria's smartphone market is expected to triple to more than 140 million by 2025[14] and the country's mobile economy is set to grow by 19 per cent between 2019 and 2025 – the highest rate in sub-Saharan Africa, which is the fastest-growing mobile technology region in the world.[15]

The GSMA is an industry organisation that represents the interests of mobile network operators worldwide. Its analysis suggests that mobile technologies and services generated 9 per cent of GDP in sub-Saharan Africa in 2019 – a contribution that amounted to more than US$132 billion of economic value. The mobile ecosystem also supported almost 1.1 million jobs.

In some areas – such as the mobile financial sector – sub-Saharan Africa has become a global leader. By the end of 2018, there were almost 396 million registered mobile money accounts in the region, representing nearly half of the global total.[16] Mobile money transactions average close to 25 per cent as a share of GDP in the region, against just 5 per cent in the rest of the world.[17]

Figure 28 Predicted growth in sub-Saharan Africa mobile industry contribution to GDP
Source: www.gsma.com/mobileeconomy/sub-saharan-africa/

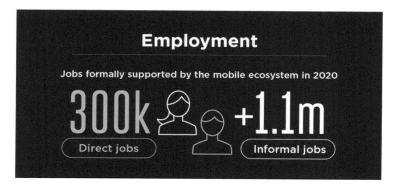

Figure 29 Sub-Saharan African jobs formally supported by the mobile industry ecosystem, 2020
Source: www.gsma.com/mobileeconomy/sub-saharan-africa/

'Today, more people in sub-Saharan Africa use mobile money than people in the rest of the world', says Catherina Hinz, director of the Berlin Institute. 'People who formerly had no access to bank accounts can now transfer and withdraw money and take out loans or insurance via mobile phone.'

Tamara Ojeaga, 39, who runs Rude Activewear in her spare time, is also chief client officer at Kantar's Insights Division in Lagos. She says: 'Banking in Nigeria is so future forward and fast moving that you don't even need cards at the ATM, just a phone code. There is even SMS banking for data-less phones. And we access everything from banking, to content, culture and entertainment through our phones. There is literally an app for everything.'

Omomi, a healthcare app developed by Nigerian doctor Charles Akhimien, is an example. It provides mothers and pregnant women with information about children's health and connects them to doctors in real time. Health provision in poor, remote rural areas is a challenge but with an app like Omomi, trained medical personnel can answer questions on common childhood illnesses within minutes and there's also an online community that allows women to share information.

Mobile telephony is just one form of technology that is enabling the continent to bypass traditional routes to development: a process known as leapfrogging. 'African countries have already taken a leap forward, leaving more developed countries behind', says Hinz. 'In Europe, for example, drones as suppliers of blood reserves or medicines are still dreams of the future; in Ghana or Rwanda they are a reality. Small buses in Nairobi offer WiFi to their customers but if you travel by bus on German country roads you can often search in vain for an internet connection. In rural areas in some African countries, they are using eco-friendly, high-tech solutions that use less water, leapfrogging the approach taken in developed nations. There are a lot of shortcuts developing countries can use and we are starting to see that.'

For the Soro Soke generation, leveraging the Fourth Industrial Revolution is about thinking big, thinking differently and unearthing unconventional approaches to reimagine Africa in a digital way. Young sub-Saharan Africans are using tech-based solutions across agriculture, education, finance, healthcare and infrastructure, sensing an opportunity to develop African economies at lower cost and faster speed.

Odionye Confidence, 27, is the founder and president of Lagos-based drone specialists Beat Drone. Most farms in sub-Saharan Africa remain dependent on manual labour. Rather than shift the sector to mechanised equipment, which is high cost, difficult to deliver to remote rural communities and has a heavy environmental footprint, Confidence believes a new technology – drones – are a better solution for African farmers.

'We met Nigerian farmers and asked them what problems they face and what eats their money', says Confidence. 'Usually it is inputs – chemicals and fertilisers – that are both the biggest cost and challenge. They have issues

Figure 30 Odionye Confidence, 27, founder and president of Beat Drone
Credit: Odionye Confidence

with accuracy: people spray too much or not enough and sometimes they don't spray in the right place. Many farmers had a chemical footprint per hectare that was too high. With drones, we are able to reduce the chemical footprint and water usage, and with better accuracy comes better yields. It also reduces costs. Drones use half the chemicals and only a tenth of the water. And a drone can do in 15 minutes what takes two people five hours. If you are flying a drone, you can be 1km away, you don't have any contact with chemicals, so it's a decent working environment, too.'

The company has seen growing demand for its services. 'We expect to have 45 drones in the air by the end of 2021. But the orders are far more than we can fulfil so we are looking to make our own drones and bring more people into the space', says Confidence.

Beat Drone is opening a drone factory: manufacturing will begin in early 2022. 'Our first Made in Nigeria drones will fly in December 2022, and we will be fully commercial in second quarter 2023', says Confidence. 'We hope

Figure 31 Beat Drone technology in agricultural use
Credit: Odionye Confidence

to produce 3,000 drones annually for the Nigerian and African market. Because we will be manufacturing here, we can deliver drones more cheaply and they will be tailored to our market, too. Every area has its own distinct way of farming, and we know very well what we need here.'

Beat Drone has also opened an academy to train drone pilots in partnership with the University of Ibadan. 'We're training people how to use the equipment because the market is huge. Once people are trained, they can run their own business, make their own money. Our plan is to lease the drone to them. They will pay back over a number of years and then they will have full ownership of the drone.'

Confidence is typical of this generation of entrepreneur – running successful businesses driven by creative disruption and focused on delivering solutions to larger problems.

'As a business founder, you have to be able to look around, see these kinds of problems, and think, how can I fix it?', says Eweniyi. 'All of the founders I know, everyone is latching on to a problem and hacking away at it. I think that's a uniquely African trait because in the West, based on Maslow's hierarchy, the problems are more abstract than the ones that we are dealing with. And we don't have a choice. No one else is going to come and fix it for us. And it's not just founders, it's all the young people in Nigeria. We have all realised that we are on our own. No one is coming. We have to fix our problems ourselves.'

Iyinoluwa Aboyeji, 31, has presided over two highly successful Nigerian companies, including talent network Andela and secure online payment system Flutterwave. He says solving social problems is not just about feeling good, it is also a way to ensure success.

'For me, like many other Nigerians who are entrepreneurial, we didn't start by trying to change the world, we were just trying to survive', he says. 'I was very focused on how much money I could make for a very long time. I wanted to prove to everybody I could make lots of money like [Mark Zuckerberg] did. But it wasn't until I got to a place in my life where I started to understand that technology represents an opportunity to serve people that I really got my big break. The big idea, the big lesson I learned from building businesses like Andela and Flutterwave, is that embedded in the challenges are the opportunities. So, take a crazy challenge like youth unemployment and turn it into an opportunity for remote working. Take an incredible challenge like financial exclusion and turn it into an opportunity for global payments. Do the things that are only possible to do here. You can still make money this way if that's what you care about. But this is about more than making money: it is a service to the country. It's about building a path to a future where prosperity is within everyone's reach.'

SPEAKING OUT: RINU ODUALA ON THE #ENDSARS PROTESTS

'There may be times when we are powerless to prevent injustice, but there must never be a time when we fail to protest.'

***

'Everybody knows the kind of country we are from. We have issues with human rights, with terrorism, with school children being kidnapped. Especially for young people, every day is about survival.

Figure 32 Rinu Oduala, 23, activist and organiser of the #endSARS movement
Credit: Rinu Oduala

It is the young generation that bears the brunt of police brutality. It is really a matter of survival. You can die here at any time. Young people instinctively know that if you are in the wrong place at the wrong time and with the wrong police, it becomes a matter of survival. The police are supposed to keep us safe, to look out for us, but instead they seek to extort from you, anything from US$1 to thousands of dollars. They will torture you to get the money and if you are really unlucky, you die.

The police generally are bad eggs, but SARS [the Special Anti-Robbery Squad police unit] are extra bad eggs. They have degenerated into criminals in uniform. They were formed to deal with robbery and kidnapping and now they are doing the kidnapping themselves. They are framing people on bogus charges and only if you have the money to pay them, you can go free.

On 20 June 2020, a 16-year-old girl was killed by a police officer. It was around the same time George Floyd was killed in the US. We saw the way mass protests built up around his death and the growth of Black Lives Matter. I met up with friends and started a protest and online petition. We were met with nonchalance from the police. They think nothing will change at the end of it all. Then in October another video came out. A man was arrested, the police drive off and the guy falls or is pushed from the van. This is not the first time this has happened. We face this kind of thing every day. There's this quote: "There may be times when we are powerless to prevent injustice, but there must never be a time when we fail to protest." So, we decided to protest again.

We decided let's sleep out on the streets. It sounds crazy but if our homes and our cars aren't safe – they can barge in your home anytime without a warrant, steal your valuables or stop you on the road, plant evidence and extort you before they let you go – if our roads and homes are not safe, let's all be out on the street.

On 7 October, we protested on the streets outside police headquarters and on 8 October, outside the State Assembly. In the middle of the night, on 8 October, we were almost killed by the police. They were pointing guns at us, and they would have shot us. It's only because we were live streaming videos that they did not.

The police action outside the State Assembly meant that the next protest really blew up across the country. We had protests in all the states. The Feminist Coalition started crowdfunding. We used all forms of technology. Twitter really amplified the protests, even Jack Dorsey, the Twitter CEO, was involved. We used Facebook, and Instagram and crowdfunding to get protestors out of prison. We used bitcoin when the Nigerian government shut down our financial accounts.

The protests grew. They got bigger and bigger. Then came 20 October.'

8 THE HASHTAG GENERATION

It is the evening of 20 October 2020. In Lagos, the skies are clear, the air is warm and hundreds of young people have gathered as part of the ongoing #endSARS movement against police brutality. They are massed in front of Lekki Tollgate, which separates Victoria Island from the Lekki Peninsula. It's the perfect place to protest. The road widens here, from two lanes to a broad space leading up to a dozen or more toll booths, making it a good place to gather. It's also strategically important: with the tolls blocked, normal traffic between the islands is disrupted.

As dusk approaches, the protestors are peaceful and cheerful. There's a festival atmosphere. Young men and women, many carrying the country's green and white flag, are singing the national anthem, laughing, dancing. Some chant 'soro soke', the phrase that has become a battle cry of the movement. Many are live streaming the moment on their mobile phones. An organiser stands on a platform. Calling for 'a peaceful protest', he is met with cheers of agreement and a sea of waving flags.

Unexpectedly, the lights above the tollgate go off. In the gloom, a series of shots ring out. There is confusion, fear. The young protestors start moving, down the road, away from the gate. More shots. Young people are lying on the ground trying to avoid bullets, several bleeding heavily, some moaning in pain. A small group tries, unsuccessfully, to revive a still body. Among the chaos and dread, live video streaming continues: 'They are shooting at us, they are shooting at us', says a voice, filming the bullet casings in her hand. According to a BBC reporter who was at the scene, there was 'continuous shooting' for at least 25 minutes before she was allowed to leave, but only after showing her press credentials.[1]

A few days later, CCTV images come to light. They show truckloads of Nigerian security forces pulling up at the tollgate. Dismounting, they move towards the peaceful protestors and some fire indiscriminately into the crowd. At first the security services will deny this happened. Later there is a partial admission, in the face of overwhelming video evidence, that some soldiers were at the scene and may have had a mix of live and blank rounds in their weapons.[2] There is confusion as to how many people have been killed. The government denies there were any fatalities; protestors, families and Amnesty International say at least 12 young people died.[3] More than a year later a specially formed judicial panel submits an official report that describes the scene as a 'massacre'.[4]

***

Twenty days before the killings, on 1 October 2020, Nigeria marks 60 years since independence from British colonial rule. It should be a time of celebration, but many young people feel far from euphoric.[5] Jobs are thin on the ground, the currency is devaluing fast, food inflation is causing further hardship, Boko Haram is a growing force in the north and bandit kidnappings are a continuous threat. The police, widely seen as incompetent at best, criminally dangerous at worst, are an added challenge rather than any kind of resource. Journalist and writer Fisayo Soyombo's tweet from that day captures the mood of many: 'Today, Nigeria's 60th Independence Day, I am sad, spent, drained, despondent, crest-fallen. And I am angry. Everything. It is Day 2 into the abduction of my bosom friend and his colleague, with a cold-blooded criminal telling me it's N100million or they will be killed today.'[6]

This despondency perhaps reflects why, one week later on 8 October, the shooting of a young man at the hands of the SARS unit,[7] filmed and shared on Twitter and other social media, has the effect of galvanising a generation. The #endSARS movement has been rumbling along for years. Allegations of brutality by the unit have been long documented and the #endSARS hashtag was first created in 2017. But growing smartphone ownership and the concurrent growth in the use of social media, along with widespread youth discontent with poor governance, means the 2020 protests achieve a mass not seen before.

'In 10 years, everything has changed for young people', says Ndeye Diagne, who heads up marketing research specialist Kantar in Nigeria and oversaw the group's continent-wide research into changing social attitudes. 'Social media is deeply entrenched and has provided access to the world like never before. It is a key change agent that has given Gen Z a unique opportunity.'

Figure 33 An #endSARS protest in Lagos in October 2020
Source: Pius Utomi Ekpei/AFP/Getty Images

As mobile internet penetration continues to grow across Africa, so has the use of social media. According to Kantar's research, in Nigeria, 75 per cent of those who have access to the Internet use social media, in particular WhatsApp, Instagram, Facebook, YouTube and Twitter. Facebook is the most visited website in Africa – as of December 2020, there were more than 233 million subscribers on the continent.[8]

Age has long been venerated across Africa and young people are traditionally deferential to older people in their family and society at large. Social media is upending this. The Soro Soke generation is using social media to push back against tradition and fight for change for causes ranging from the climate crisis to police brutality, sexual abuse and minority rights. For this generation, social media is also a megaphone that amplifies their political thoughts. A survey among people aged 15–34 in Ghana, Kenya, Nigeria, South Africa and Uganda finds that two-thirds of those surveyed are posting about politics.[9]

'Social media has given young people new ways of interacting and new expectations of how it's possible to live', says Diagne. 'Gen Z are able to speak out about their frustrations, they are not afraid to try and change things. They are more fearless even than the millennial generation right before them. They use technology to speak their truth. They see how things work in other parts of the world and they want things to change here. The things older generations have lived with and tolerated, younger generations want to change, and they believe it can change.'

Climate activist Olumide Idowu, 29, founded Climate Wednesday on Twitter in 2013. 'I haven't missed a Wednesday since we started', he says. 'Every week we hold a video conversation and it's also available on Facebook and YouTube. We talk to people about climate justice and how they can fight for their environmental rights. Each month it's a different topic – for example, we did a month on agriculture, where we covered how farmers can be more environmentally friendly and we covered topics like GMO crops.'

Twitter has enabled Idowu to spread the climate message across Nigeria and West Africa. 'Maybe we can't come and meet you in your state or your country, but we can share our knowledge on social media. People are live sharing, people are watching from everywhere, and it's a real-time discussion.'

Cross-border engagement is significant, says Nigerian writer Ayo Sogunro, because while African leaders have always had spaces for cross-continental conversations, ordinary Africans have rarely had such opportunities.[10] '[I]n a continent where opportunities for international engagement between everyday people is severely limited, social media provides a space – for increasing numbers of Africans though far from all – to connect, to redefine African values, to recognise shared inequities and ambitions, and to stand up against authoritarianism, racism, patriarchy, injustice, and other daily discriminations', Sogunro writes.[11]

Professor Alcinda Honwana is a Mozambican anthropologist and Centennial Professor at the London School of Economics. A leading scholar on youth-led protests in Africa, she has studied movements across the continent – from a drive for greater local government representation in Tunisia to a hip-hop-led movement raising political awareness in Angola. She points to the power of social media in enabling comparison and in driving change by offering this generation a level of pan-African and global connectivity that has never been possible before. Speaking at her 2021 University of Oxford Annual Africa Studies lecture, she said: 'The internet has enabled comparison with other lives and the contradictions can feel intolerable', she says.

Influencer and entrepreneur John Obidi, 34, voices the same sentiment. 'Social media is our window to the world', he says. 'Now we can connect globally and see how alike we are globally too. We can see global trends; we can identify as global human beings. Before Twitter, we had only one version of democracy. Now we can see what Germans or Americans, or Iraqis or Afghanis think about democracy. We don't just base our world view on our lives, but how people live in other places also. In Nigeria we don't have a big tradition of protest but in 2020 we saw protests against bad governance and police brutality. I think that was influenced by what we saw with Black Lives Matter and other movements abroad. Without social media we wouldn't have seen the models operating in other places.'

Diagne calls Gen Z 'the hashtag generation'. 'They believe that #AfricaMatters. From #endSARS to #FixGhana-Now, they are using social media to disrupt, to surprise

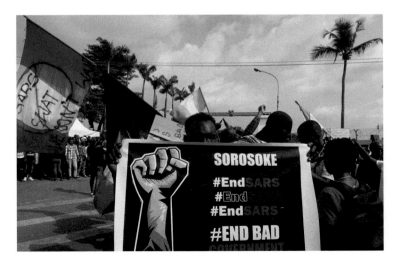

Figure 34 An #endSARS protest in Lagos in October 2020
Source: NurPhoto/Getty Images

and to change Africa for the better', she says. 'And because of the size of the cohort they are starting to be taken seriously.'

***

Osinachi, 30, is a successful artist. Slight in build, he wears his hair close to his head in short, neat dreadlocks. When we meet, he's dressed in a traditionally cut suit in a simple white fabric. He is stylish, and his demeanour is confident yet also unassuming. He seems an unlikely target for police profiling but says he's regularly been the victim of police harassment. 'As a young person, I can't just drive out of my house and believe I won't be harassed by the police', he says. 'They profile me because I have dreads and drive an SUV and they try to rip me off. It's crazy. This is what led to the #endSARS protests. There was so much profiling and extortion of young people. The system is entirely broken.'

Photographer Uzor, 28, agrees. 'Every single young person has a story about the police. There is no one who doesn't understand, no one who hasn't had some problem', he says. 'Armed robbers take you, walk you to the bank and make you withdraw your money. Then the police come, take you and walk you to the bank and make you withdraw all your money. Tell me, what is the difference between them?'

Rinu Oduala, 23, a key organiser of the protests, says young women also face harassment. 'It is not just young males. Females bear the brunt of police brutality. We are raped, tortured and killed.' Perhaps because of this, as the #endSARS protests gather pace, an organising committee emerges formed largely of young women from a group called the Feminist Coalition. The women establish a 24-hour helpline that people can call in emergencies, they provide legal services to those in need and even set up a radio station. Funmi Oyatogun, 29, is part of the committee. 'At one stage we had to tell people only to call the helpline about #endSARS issues, we were getting calls asking for our help with all sorts of things', she says.

All of the group's costs are met by fundraising. The women release a publicly accessible, daily summary of their accounts, showing the amounts received and how it is being disbursed.[12] When the government freezes the committee's bank account, the group continues raising funds using cryptocurrency.

'Women are at the heart of the 2020 #endSARS movement', says Oduala. 'And with the presence of women, the dynamic changed. The strong women of Feminist Coalition raised US$400,000 and used it to feed protestors, to pay for ambulances and pay legal costs and to provide mental health support. It was accountable and very effective. I believe it showcased and helped us visualise what a future Nigeria could look like with good governance, transparency and accountability.'

Figure 35 Rinu Oduala speaks at an #endSARS protest in Lagos in October 2020
Source: Pius Utomi Ekpei/AFP/Getty Images

Oduala's point is echoed by others. The organisers' high level of accountability – something sorely missing from the country's moribund public sector institutions and from government at all levels – helped drive the popularity of the movement, even across older age groups. Tamara Ojeaga, 39, did not take part in the protests but as she watched events unfold she found the transparency and organisation inspiring. 'The organisation was next level', she says. 'They used bitcoin and cryptocurrency for donations and were fully transparent in reporting where donations were spent. They made it obvious that this country can actually work if we want it to. It gave me such hope.'

The organising committee also uses social media extensively: to call young people to action, to fundraise and to bring the issue to global attention. By October 2020, 48 million #endSARS tweets are posted in just 10 days.[13] Engagement with the cause comes from around the world – Twitter founder Jack Dorsey tweets in support and the company also designs a logo, a fist wrapped in the Nigerian flag, for the movement.

The majority of Nigeria's mainstream media outlets – which have close links to government officials and the Nigerian state – give the #endSARS movement little or no coverage.[14] But this has limited impact. Young Nigerians, like others in their cohort around the world, largely ignore mainstream media outlets and instead turn to social media for information. During #endSARS it becomes clear that the future of activism across the continent and the growth of youthful participation in politics and civil society are directly linked to the ability of activists to amplify their causes across social media platforms. 'Social media has created a unique kind of space that is not subject to the physical control of the military or police', writes Sogunro. 'If African activists can utilise this space effectively, they can play a major part in shaping African society for the next generation.'[15]

Threatened by the power of platforms such as Twitter, the frequency and duration of internet shutdowns by governments across Africa is steadily increasing.[16] In June 2021, the Nigerian government suspended Twitter in the country, ostensibly because the platform deleted a tweet by President Buhari that it deemed abusive. Most young Nigerians believe the deleted tweet was a much-sought-after excuse for a ban that had been on the cards since the rise of the #endSARS protest movement.

'Since the government suspended Twitter in Nigeria, the coordination and organisation of the movement has been a bit restrained', says Oduala. 'Twitter was one of the last places where we could express ourselves. Closing it down was a way for the government to target mass movements organised by young Nigerians. They saw the ability of social media platforms to help organise protests and so they closed it down.'

Technology entrepreneur Iyinoluwa Aboyeji, 31, believes the political establishment is threatened by the financial and organisational freedom that technology more broadly offers young people. 'We have been very much attacked as an industry by the political establishment because of the challenge we represent to their power', he says. 'When we can take someone's income from 40,000 naira (US$80) to US$80,000 in a two and a half year period, it is very dangerous to the establishment. That was what #endSARS was really about – it was a challenge to the establishment by people who could finance their own revolution. And that made everyone in power worried and scared. Especially because the protestors were leveraging modern technology tools, which made it very difficult to stop the machine.'

***

As October 2020 progresses, the machine powers on and the movement grows daily. Protests spread from Lagos across the country, including to Abuja, the capital. The government begins to take notice. It's clear that someone feels threatened. On 20 October, the shootings take place.

'There is a huge division between politicians and youth', says Ojeaga. 'It's generational and attitudinal. Today's politicians are ex-military and it's either their way or the highway. There is an oppression mentality at the top.'

'The government was scared, they were shaking, they were worried about what might happen if we continued', says Oyatogun. 'Our president said that young people were trying to unseat him. But we were not. We just want to feel safe. We were naïve. We didn't think they would actually shoot at us, kill us. The older ones with long memories, they warned us, they remember from before how it can be.'

After the shootings, the movement comes off the streets. The government freezes the bank accounts of key activists, some have their passport seized. Several activists leave the country in fear. 'The shootings broke something in us. They were traumatic, and many haven't recovered from the experience', says Oduala. 'Some young Nigerians are living in fear for their lives. People like DJ Switch, who was at the height of her career, are leaving the country. My personal bank account was frozen, and my passport was seized, along with those of 19 others. We had to have legal tussles with the government to overturn these things.'

A judicial enquiry into the shootings is convened. 'I was the youngest person on the judicial panel looking into the shootings', says Oduala. 'It brought me face to face with how the government works, with criminals in police uniforms, with the broken judiciary system. Hearing the horrors that people went through, of so many lives and families ruined forever by policemen who are still in service today was a traumatic experience.'

In November 2021 the judicial panel releases its report. It finds that the army 'shot, injured and killed unarmed, helpless and defenceless protesters, without provocation or justification', conduct that was exacerbated by 'its refusal to allow ambulances [to] render medical assistance to victims who required such assistance'. It also alleges cover-up attempts: 'The police officers also tried to cover up their actions by picking up bullets', the report says, and it goes on to accuse Nigerian authorities of tampering with CCTV footage and removing the bodies of the dead from the scene.[17]

Although the report recommends that those involved in the Lekki Tollgate shootings face 'appropriate disciplinary action and be stripped of their status' before being dismissed, to date no one has faced prosecution or accepted responsibility for the killings. There is no clarity on who ordered the security services to confront the protestors or who authorised the shootings.

***

Although #endSARS may be off the streets, youth discontent rumbles on, and not just in Nigeria. As Honwana points out: a new wave of global social movements is being led by young Africans. In the same way that a wave of European Baby Boomers took to the streets demanding social change as teenagers and young adults in the student protests of 1968, this cohort of young Africans are at the forefront of similar protests. Speaking at the 2021 University of Oxford Annual Africa Studies lecture, Honwana said: 'From Tunisia and Egypt to Senegal and Angola, young people are fighting for a greater political voice, for access to job opportunities and for broader systemic change'.

Some 93 per cent of Gen Z respondents to Kantar's Africa Life survey in five countries across sub-Saharan Africa agree with the statement 'our society needs a common purpose'. 'Young people believe that standing for something is essential and they want to stand for something bigger than themselves', says Diagne. 'They are also looking for real leadership and are seeing and celebrating new heroes, such Emma Theofelus of Namibia, the continent's youngest minister in government at 23.'

In Nigeria, #endSARS is the country's most significant protest movement since pro-democracy rallies in the 1990s, and for many young Nigerians it constituted a real political awakening. The protests brought recognition that young people could be a powerful political force, combined with the more brutal insight that the establishment will respond violently to perceived challenges. And there is a growing belief among this cohort that it is young people who will build the country they are looking for.

'I think young people have the power to make things better despite the government. The #endSARS protests are a testament to that. Despite the massacre, it was really impactful. These guys at the top saw the power of young people coming together', says Osinachi.

Nigeria is vast and heterogeneous, composed of different religions and different ethnicities and successive governments have used a strategy of dividing to conquer, setting different interest groups against each other. The #endSARS movement, in contrast, united young people across ethnic and religious divides. 'The movement brought people together from across regions and across religions and gave us a new-found sense of unity', says Oduala. 'It is a spirit that binds young Nigerians. We are doing things differently. We are having frank conversations about the rights of people with disabilities, about LGQBT rights. We have put aside tribal and religious differences. This sentiment sets us apart from older generations.'

Another factor that distinguishes this generation is their coming of age during a time of democracy – only a few are old enough to properly remember Nigeria's period of military rule, which ended in 1999 – and their rejection of the existing political class, which even today contains many members of the pre-democracy juntas.[18]

'There were civil wars and dictators in the lifetime of the older generation that really limited how they were able to express themselves', says 32-year-old Michael Elégbèdé.

'Even today, if you look at #endSARS, our own government killed us with no repercussion. That was the norm in the past. But that's not going to stop this generation. They are trying to use the old ways, to bring us into line with abuse and threats. But it is not working. And it's not going to work. And that's what is differentiating this generation from the past.'

There is a growing perception among young Nigerians that street-led protests are not enough on their own and that young politicians need to become a part of the system in order to change it from within. Tonye Isokariari, 34, has been involved in politics since 2010, when he was part of the Goodluck Jonathan presidential campaign. 'For the first time, during the #endSARS protests, the government was jittery over young people's involvement. If we can come together like that across the board, we can take back our country', says Isokariari. 'We need to gather a lot of young people who have shown capacity, who have shown they are there to serve, so that we can change the system from within. A lot of times when you are outside making noise, nothing happens. We have to do it from inside, stirring the water from within.'

The challenge moving forward will be to see if this moment of activism and protest can be translated into a long-term political movement. 'We could have done a lot more', says 25-year-old activist S. I. Ohumu. 'It's understanding that shouting is not the only thing. There is a social change system and everyone has a role to play. There are the disruptors, the people who love Twitter and make a lot of noise and go to protest. But that is only the first step. We also need mediators who are willing to compromise. People who are able to build bridges. Compromise is not necessarily a bad word.'

Ibrahim Faruk, 35, is programme manager at the Youth Initiative for Advocacy, Growth and Advancement (YIAGA), a non-profit organisation based in Abuja that promotes good governance and aims to increase youth participation. He agrees with Ohumu that greater engagement with the political system is needed. 'There are conversations that need to be had with the National Human Rights Commission, with the Police Service Commission, organisations like that', he says. 'If you are not sitting at the table, you are just making noise from the outside and while that is very important it's also important to engage with the systems and institutions. It's something that many young people don't like to do, or don't want to do because they have lost trust in those organisations. But how else can we get these institutions to reform if we do not engage one way or another?'

Ohumu concedes that politics and corruption are synonymous in Nigeria but says 'it's time to get over that'. 'If young people don't get into those spaces, we will not innovate out of a bad situation', she says. 'We young people are plenty and we are building wealth, so we can fund things, too. If we can fund #endSARS we can fund elections. It's a matter of political will. We just have to be interested.'

Oduala is confident that change is coming. 'Before the shootings, we had begun to hope for a new Nigeria. A Nigeria where young people have a seat at the table of power, a Nigeria where young people can walk free on the streets, a Nigeria where the common man can get justice', she says. 'The fight might be off the streets and off the TV, but it hasn't stopped or lost importance. Young Nigerians are very stubborn and don't give up. #endSARS is a movement not a moment and our hearts are still in the movement. We are not backing down. We will take every avenue available to enact the change we want and deserve – we will vote, we will go to the street, we will use social media. We are fighting for system change and justice. We are showcasing that we can bring about change and we are enacting the kind of change we seek.'

SPEAKING OUT: PRINCESS OBIAJULU UGWU ON STANDING FOR ELECTION

'I contested elections as a form of protest to the existing leadership, in which nothing seems to be working out. It wasn't an easy feat especially as a young female candidate.'

Figure 36 Princess Obiajulu Ugwu, 37, ran for a seat in the Enugu State House of Assembly at the 2019 General Election
Credit: Princess Obiajulu Ugwu

'In the 2019 elections, when I was 35, I contested for a seat in the Enugu State House of Assembly under the United Progressive Party. There was no sponsorship from the party aside from giving free nomination forms to women and youth. Most of my support came from family, friends and colleagues who have seen my passion and believed in my ability to handle leadership positions and deliver change.

I contested as a form of protest to the existing leadership, in which nothing seems to be working out. It wasn't an easy feat especially as a young female candidate. Some in society saw me as a deviant and called me a prostitute. Even some family members said I was overstepping my boundaries and should be stopped before I disgraced them. Men who were in the race tried to discourage me. I was sold out by a member of my party who felt a male candidate from another party, contesting the same position, was a better option. He asked me to step down and, when I declined, he started campaigning against me. One of the other major challenges I faced was finance. During the campaign period, we went out to speak to people, but they wouldn't listen if we had nothing to put on the table.

I do not intend to call this my biggest achievement in politics because it was just a foundation and, by God's grace, I will keep trying to find a space to dish out all that is deposited in me to help humanity. But I will say I have gained visibility and also insight into how the system is run, which is unpleasant.

I am sharing my story because I believe it can reawaken sleeping giants in some of the female folk around Africa and the globe into realising their full potential, especially as it concerns leadership and politics.'

SPEAKING OUT: FORTUNES ORONKWO ON THE MONETISATION OF POLITICS

'*My party, the Progressive People's Congress, despite being a new party founded on a strong political ideology, did not win a single seat, largely due to financial constraints and its unwillingness to play outside the rules of the game.*'

'*I belong to a society that sees youth as the leaders of tomorrow, not of today. Rather than encourage youth involvement in politics and nation building, the older generation sees us as tools that can be used to foster their interests and achieve their political goals. This phenomenon has, over time, disempowered the most active and vibrant population in our society.*

Contesting the 2019 governorship was an eye-opener for me. I became aware of the intrigues involved in winning an election as well as the humongous amount of money needed throughout the electioneering period. Presently in Nigeria there are two major political parties, and these two parties control the dynamics of who wins what. So, contesting an election outside these two parties poses great challenge. My party, the Progressive People's Congress, despite being founded on a strong political ideology, did not win a single seat, largely due to financial constraints and its unwillingness to play outside the rules of the game.

Inadequate funding posed the greatest challenge. Winning an election in Nigeria is capital intensive. There are financial benchmarks set by the country's election umpire but the major

Figure 37 Fortunes Paul Okoronkwo, 39,
contested the governorship election in
his home state of Abia for the Progressive
People's Congress in 2019
Credit: Fortunes Paul Okoronkwo

*political parties and their candidates are known to spend way
beyond these, thereby significantly narrowing the chances of the
smaller political parties. Unfortunately, none of our candidates,
including myself, could match the financial fire power of our op-
ponents and our best efforts and ideas were scuttled due to lack
of funding. Not many people were willing to pay attention to our
manifesto once it was obvious we weren't going to dole out cash after each campaign. So, to a large extent, the election was lost even
before the first vote was cast.*

There is also a high cost to securing nomination forms, especially for the major parties. To get on these parties' nomination forms, an aspirant must be rich. Since not many youths can afford it, contesting on the platforms of relatively unknown political parties becomes the only option for people like me. Even to secure my party's governorship nomination form, I paid a quarter of a million naira (approx US$600).

In the end, I emerged as the sole candidate from my party for the governorship and came fifth out of the 31 candidates that contested the election. It was not a bad start, the financial and cultural challenges notwithstanding.

In hindsight, I will say my biggest achievement has been learning that it takes creativity, ingenuity and a sense of mission and purpose to contest an election as a young person and to remain in the race till the end. I have also learnt that young people seeking elective positions must stay true to their guiding principles. Without that it is quite easy to either get discouraged or get influenced to join the bandwagon of politrickians.'

9   CONTESTING
FOR POWER

'There is one issue that threatens us: bad governance. No matter how you look at it, everything comes back to that. We don't have leaders that are accountable, we don't have leaders that are competent, we don't have leaders that are motivated or have the political will to change things. We don't have people for whom there is a future. We have old people who only care about how much of the common wealth they are able to steal while we suffer.' S. I., 25

'Who are the people making decisions for young people? Can they even relate to us? Are they up to date with tech or are they stuck in the analogue age? There are people in our government who can't handle a smartphone but think they can implement policies that young people need. They say young people have no experience, but we know better than they what we need. We need more young people in positions of policy making or influencing the policy makers. We need to either be one of the decision makers or we need to be one of the people influencing the decision makers. If they won't give us a seat at the table, we will create our own seats to be there.' Rinu, 23

'Nigerian youths are clearly saying enough is enough. We want to have the power. I'm a very fresh politician. I was appointed in February 2021. I happen to be one of the youngest members of the National Working Committee of my party, the ADC. This is one of the top positions in the party. The committee is about 30 people but 90 per cent are men and women in their 60s and 70s; there are only the three of us who are young. And when we are presenting an idea, they are not in

the same realm as we are. There is a clash of understanding. Nigerian politics is about money. Older politicians are always thinking about how they are going to pay people, and they cripple the implementation of ideas.' Ìfénlá, 33

'Our church wanted to build a better road, but the government said no because they didn't benefit from it financially. And a local NGO wanted to build a school, but the elders said they had to be paid money first. That is the problem of our country – it is all about give me my share. They don't care about development; they are more concerned if they are making money out of it. I think it's only 50/50 if younger people will be different. A lot of our generation want to get in there and share the national cake and the truth is that most average people are not exposed enough to demand more. We need politicians who are there to serve not to be served. And for the youth revolution to come we need to come together beyond our different ideology.' Uzor, 28

'Recently I've started having conversations across the political divide. The challenge in front of us is not which party someone belongs to. For now, I'm not looking at a young person in the opposition party as a problem – we are colleagues in the fight to take over our country. For young people who have shown capacity, who are ready to deliver results, let's take over. And how do we take over our country? By being sure that we are speaking one language across all parties.' Tonye, 34

'We definitely need better leaders. We need people who are aware that what they are supposed to be doing is in service to the people, and historically we haven't had a lot of that. We can only hope that as we move forward, we are able to get better leaders, people that are there to serve, make the economy stronger and deliver on the hope that Nigerians have been holding since independence. I hope younger people step up to take their own place and I hope they do it for the right reason.' Odunayo, 28

***

After the frenetic energy of Lagos, Abuja is an oasis of calm. Surrounded by forest-covered hills and defined by a series of prominent squat monoliths, Nigeria's capital is a planned city, built in the 1980s to a master plan designed by Japanese architect Kenzo Tange. The wide streets and avenues of the city centre are lined with government offices, the gold-domed Nigeria National Mosque and the postmodern neo-Gothic National Christian Centre. Five-star hotels, banks and shopping malls sit beside large mansions that house ministers and notables.

At the heart of the city is Circular Road. It surrounds the officially named Three Arms Zone, so-named because it houses the three arms of government – the Supreme Court, the National Assembly and the Presidential villa – locals simply call the whole zone the Villa. The area is imposing, forbidding even. CCTV cameras proliferate on the high fence that surrounds the compound. Every 10 yards along the pavement, signs are stencilled in red paint: no stopping, no parking, no waiting. Concrete bollards and armed guards line the entry road. The effect is of a walled-off elite, a government protecting itself from the people it is supposed to represent.

Africa may be home to the youngest population on earth, but its leaders are among the oldest. Many are in their 80s; President Robert Mugabe of Zimbabwe was 93 when he was ousted in 2017. In 2015, the median age across sub-Saharan Africa was 19, while the median age of executive office holders was 64, a gap of 45 years.[1] In contrast, in the member states of the OECD there is a gap of only 12 years between leaders and the electorate. There is a long history of protest and activism by young Africans: Steve Biko and Patrice Lumumba were not old men. In Nigeria, Nnandi Azikiwe was still in his 30s when he founded the National Council of Nigeria and the Cameroons in 1944. Others, including Obafemi Awolowo and Samuel Akintola rose to prominence during the struggle for independence in the 1950s and 1960s.[2] But after that, youth involvement in nation building slowed and, across much of Africa, ruling elites have remained entrenched for decades. At the end of 2018, 15 African executive office holders had been in power for more than 10 years, with an average of 24 years in office.[3] In 2020, three sitting African heads of state had been in power for more than three decades each.

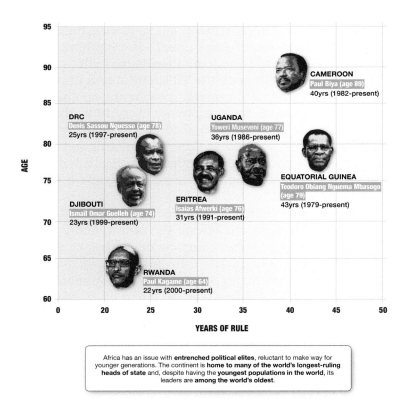

Figure 38 African presidents who have been in power for over 20 years
Created by Russell Henry Design

Nigerian president, Muhammadu Buhari, 78, who was elected in 2015, is in this mould. An ex-military officer – he was previously head of state in the 1980s, when he took power in a military coup d'état – Buhari has been in and around the top echelons of power for more than 40 years. A 'big man' in the African style, his fealty is to tradition and the ongoing support of a vast network of cohorts. Many Nigerians are angry that they see so little benefit from the country's billions of petrodollars, much of which has been squandered or stolen,[4] and Buhari was elected on his reputation for fighting corruption. But he has had little effect on the rampant misuse of government positions and funds and has been accused of cronyism and politicking in those cases that have been pursued.[5] Buhari also seems woefully out of touch with his young electorate. In 2016 he accused young Nigerians of criminality and in 2018 of being lazy and uneducated.[6]

But, as the West Africa Centre for Democracy and Development notes, far from being frivolous and lazy, young Nigerians have simply lost hope in institutions that do not serve their interests.[7] The majority of Africans, and especially young Africans, think their governments are doing a very bad or a fairly bad job at addressing the needs of

Figure 39 Nigeria's president, Muhammadu Buhari
Source: Pool/Getty Images

the youth.[8] In five out of seven African countries surveyed in 2017 (Egypt, Ghana, Morocco, Nigeria, South Africa) at least 75 per cent of young people said their governments did not care about their needs.[9] This has led to disenfranchisement. According to Afrobarometer, the percentage of respondents who voted in their country's last election is 14 percentage points lower for young Africans (aged 18–35) than for those over 35. And almost one in 10 young Africans say they deliberately decided not to vote.[10]

'Some young people are galvanised', says Rinu Oduala, 23. 'For the upcoming 2023 election, 80 per cent of newly registered voters are young people. But many others are still marginalised. There's an apathy in the country, people don't feel they need to vote. They don't see any result from their votes. The government doesn't seem to do anything; it's a government for the elite not the masses so people don't see a need to participate.'

Counter-intuitively, it may be this disillusionment that represents the best opportunity to reshape political participation. In the months after the president's derogatory comments, the hashtag #LazyNigeriaYouth went viral – a backlash that, according to market research specialist Canvas8, shows a growing political engagement among young Nigerians.[11] An August 2020 report by the group says: 'So wide is the disconnect between those in government and the public, that change seems almost inevitable.'[12]

***

While the centre of Abuja, with its walled-off and architecturally imposing buildings, emits the aura of a sealed-off elite, the city's suburbs feel much more egalitarian and energetic. On a weekday lunchtime, the thriving middle-class neighbourhood of Gwarimpa is busy. Streets buzz with traffic: kekes and buses, cars and scooters. Markets are filled with shoppers and the roadside *Mama-puts*, small outdoor restaurants run by redoubtable older women, are bustling with lunchtime trade. Cafés and bars are busy, too. In one, on a colourful, plant-filled open balcony that overlooks a neighbourhood of pleasant suburban streets and a high, forested hill, a group of young community organisers are eating beef and rice dotted with spicy red and green chillies and discussing politics.

Jude Feranmi, 29, is the convener of the Raising New Voices Initiative, a volunteer-led non-profit committed to raising new leaders for Nigeria. He was also formerly the National Youth Caucus Leader of the KOWA party. 'I became actively involved in politics after the 2015 election', he says. 'For young people, it is a justice conversation, a prosperity conversation. It is about wanting Nigeria to be better and wanting to get involved in whatever makes it better. But it is strictly a political power conversation when it comes to older politicians. They know what they want, they will do anything to get power and they have the resources to deploy to get it. And those two positions are in conflict.'

Tonye Isokariari, 34, has been involved in Nigerian politics for more than a decade. 'The Breath of Fresh Air campaign for Goodluck Jonathan, that was me', he says. 'Some people still call me Fresh Air in political circles.' He echoes Feranmi's point. 'The process of change needs to be driven from the youth up. The older guys don't give a rat's arse. It's about personal interest for them. They are not talking about Nigeria as a country. They are talking about their personal interest and how it affects them.'

'The whole system is programmed to keep us where we are. It is an intentional effort', says Kingsley Atang, 37, programme lead at the Youth Alive Foundation, a not-for-profit focused on redefining the role and contributions of the Nigerian youth in governance. 'The political class benefits from the consequences of hunger, in that it keeps people dependent on them. People in Nigeria don't under-stand what a social contract is. They don't understand that the primary responsibility of the government is the wel-fare and security of the people.'

Feranmi agrees. The biggest problem, he says, is that Nigerian politics is seen as largely transactional. There is very limited focus on policy. 'With political power today, you can obviously see that there is a transaction going on: you give me political power and I give you money or I give you patronage. The transaction ends at the point of voting. The political dynamics do not evolve into a social contract. But I'm an idealist. I don't believe that we have to embrace what is happening right now. In politics, it is always difficult to cut away the ladder that gets you there. Not mirroring the status quo, that is the way our genera-tion will make things different.'

Student leader Olumide Areo, 26, is slim and dapper in a suit and tie. He believes it's a question of education. 'The electorate is not aware that it is their right to ask ques-tions or be given information', he says. 'Most people don't understand the nexus between politics, policy and quality of life. They do not see that they are voting for a person who makes policies that affect them. We need people to understand that they need to vote for someone who is pushing for laws that work for them.'

He gives an example: 'There were a lot of corrupt prac-tices in my school, in 2018, with large sums of money be-ing syphoned away by student leaders. But this one guy stood up and said he wanted to do something different. He wanted to prove that student presidents were not always the same. He decided to do a town hall meeting with all the students, and to ensure all the budgets for capital and expenditure were open to everyone. And he did it. I could see students begin to become aware that it is our right to understand what is going on. I could see students asking the questions and taking up the challenge, they began to own the process and challenge leaders.'

***

Areo, Atang, Feranmi and Isokariari are part of a thriving civic society based in Abuja. The city is home to a host of non-profit groups, staffed by optimistic young people – idealists and realists, side by side – facilitating everything from promoting good governance and increased transparency to increasing young voter registration and mentoring the leaders of tomorrow. And at the heart of this group is YIAGA Africa. Its offices, a two-storey building in Gwarimpa, exude purposefulness. Young activists debate issues, write reports, run information campaigns, lobby for change and work tirelessly to increase youth participation across the country. One highlight of the group's advocacy is the Not Too Young To Run bill, which was passed by the country's National Assembly in 2018. The bill saw the Nigerian constitution amended to reduce the age for presidential candidates from 40 to 35 and for House of Representatives candidates from 30 to 25 years.

'Before this, we did not have young people in elected office, no representatives in Parliament and our issues were treated with levity', says the YIAGA Africa senior programme officer, Yetunde Bakare, 33. 'When Not Too Young To Run was first proposed 10 years ago it wasn't taken seriously. We were told to sit down, it's not the time, we were not serious enough. But we built a movement and reduced the age for participation in the State Assembly and House of Representatives. Now we can participate, not only as voters but in the electoral process.'

Bakare believes its ageing Parliament is the country's biggest challenge to good governance. 'I like to refer to our Senate as a retirement home for governors', she says. 'Look at the number of past governors who are now in the

Senate – they stay there for eight years and then retire. They are not contributing to national discourse, because for them it's just a pre-retirement, wealth-generating thing. That impacts on the quality of the legislation that comes out of Parliament. I would like to see the elimination of all past politicians. If you've ever run for office before, it's over. The governors that are being recycled as senators, no! We want new faces. Our civil service also needs an overhaul. It is the engine room of any government; they remain once the executive tenure expires. But we have directors who have been in place for more than 25 years who are resistant to change and don't want to see change because the current system is benefiting them. We need to bring in new people, people who genuinely want to do the work.'

As a result of the Not Too Young To Run bill, youth candidacy was at 34 per cent in the 2019 elections[13] with 151 young candidates standing for election and five winning seats. 'One is now the speaker of a state assembly, others are whips and deputy whips and majority leaders', says Bakare. But despite this success, overall youth participation in government remains very low, with some estimates suggesting only 1 per cent of lawmakers are aged under 30.[14] In part the issue is cultural.

Chinemerem Onuorah is 25. 'There is a problem, in that people by default believe that young people are not ready to rule', she says. 'People think you are not qualified for something just because of your age and they forget the fact that the president we have today was very young when he first ruled Nigeria. So why do they think young people cannot carry on with democracy now? I feel like there are a lot of young people who have the competence and capacity to rule Nigeria and we should not disqualify them just because our cultural mentality says young people aren't ready.'

A second YIAGA Africa campaign, Ready To Run, has been launched to address this issue. 'Ready To Run was born because of the imbedded narrative that young people are not ready for public office', says Bakare. 'It responds to the need of young people who want to contest and win elections and aims to help young people perform excellently in office. It's not that we want everyone to run – we want to find young people of character, with the competence and the capacity to run. We help them mobilise issue-based campaigns and improve their chances of election.'

Alongside cultural norms, there are systemic barriers that make it difficult for young people to be elected. It is not possible to run as an independent candidate in Nigeria, and to be nominated by a party requires paying large fees and getting the support of the party's power cabal, a group often hidden from public view. Even when political

Figure 40 Some of the YIAGA Africa team (L–R): Ibrahim Faruk, 35, Yetunde Bakare, 33, and Sanusi Olaniyan, 33
Credit: Fati Abubakar

parties hold primaries to secure candidates for election, the result is often overruled if a preferred candidate is not chosen.

YIAGA programme manager Ibrahim Faruk, 35, says one of the biggest problems is that political parties themselves are undemocratic and opaque. 'There is no Nigerian party that can claim it is people owned', he says. 'In other countries, parties make efforts to attract members and the members pay dues and have a stake in the party. They contribute to decision making and in selecting candidates. We don't have that in Nigeria. Nigerian parties are owned by a few big men and what they dictate is what the party does. They shape the party. There is campaigning going on behind doors, within conclaves, within small circles of big men. They decide who will run and everyone falls behind whatever the leaders decide.'

Monetisation is a further barrier. In a blogpost for the LSE, Dr Angela Ajodo-Adebanjoko, an associate professor at the Federal University of Lafia, cites leadership deficits, poor internal democracy among political parties and the absence of a strategic political agenda as ongoing barriers for young people.[15] But, in particular, she says, there are large financial obstacles to running for office in Nigeria.

In the run-up to the 2019 general election, the cost of nomination forms for office ranged from 45 million naira (US$125,000) for presidential aspirants to 3.8 million (US$10,500) for the House of Representatives candidates.[16] Because few young Nigerians are able to afford these sums and donors usually prefer older candidates whom they believe have a higher chance of success, young people remain disenfranchised, says Dr Ajodo-Adebanjoko. 'While in theory they are Not Too Young To Run, in practice, the youth find themselves Too-Poor-To-Run', she writes.[17]

Sanusi Olaniyan, 33, is a programme assistant at YIAGA Africa and he agrees with Ajodo-Adebanjoko. 'The biggest challenge for young candidates is financial inequality', he says. 'Nigerian politics is very monetised. If you don't have a large pool of resources to draw from it is very hard to contest an election, and almost impossible to contest in an established political party.'

Michael Odoh, 30, wants to run for office. 'I was a party member for 10 years and I paid my dues to the party, in all the ways you could think of. But when I went to the party chairman and said I wanted to contest an election, he told me to wait. He said that I'm still too young and I should wait another five years. Then when he saw I was making moves, he told me I was disqualified. I left the party and joined another party but was short of the cost of registering as a candidate. You begin to understand how disenfranchised young people are.'

Garnering nomination is only the first financial barrier in the electioneering process. Vote buying is also endemic – once candidates are on the ticket, there is an expectation that they will pay key voting blocks for support. 'People who run for office have to visit traditional and religious rulers', explains Faruk. 'And they are not just going to visit empty handed. They go with a gift or with cash and they hand out salt or rice or noodles. To them that is campaigning, and it does influence whether some people vote for them. The deeper problem is that many communities do not feel a government presence. They don't have electricity, there's no water in the pipes, the roads are run down, the healthcare centres are horrible. They feel this is the only time they will see a politician and are able to benefit, so they will take what they can get.'

'You definitely find people voting for whoever can give them the most money', agrees Bakare. 'Vote selling is illegal but it's not enforced and, due to poverty, it remains part of the electoral process. If you are offered money to vote, you sell your vote to the highest bidder.'

The legislation that bans vote selling and which also sets campaign-funding limits – at one billion naira for a presidential candidate – is not well enforced. 'Campaign financing is very opaque', says Faruk. 'Political parties are supposed to report how much they spend, but in the 2019 elections, only three parties out of 91 did that. What makes it worse is that the current review of the act seeks to increase the amount for presidential campaigning to five billion naira. The election basically goes to the highest bidder.'

'How many people can afford to spend five billion naira to contest for the highest office in the land?' asks Bakare. 'It is a real challenge. Especially now that vote buying and selling is done in the open, without any fear of prosecution or arrest, because no one is monitoring electoral spending or punishing those who are in infringement of the law. People who are genuinely interested in governing, who can make a change for the country but do not have access to the funding, cannot contest for office. That's a threat to democracy.'

Nigeria is currently experiencing its longest period of civilian government since achieving independence from British colonial rule in 1960. From the 1960s to 1999, military juntas of varying openness and brutality dominated the country's politics. In 1999, the 4th Nigerian Republic was born, with the Peoples Democratic Party (PDP) elected as the governing party. Both the 2003 and 2007 presidential elections were marred by irregularities and violence, but national and state elections in 2011 and 2015 were generally regarded as credible. The 2015 election was heralded for the fact that the then opposition party, the All Progressives Congress (APC), defeated the PDP, which had governed since 1999. When current president Buhari assumed the role in 2015, it marked the country's first peaceful transfer of power from one party to another. Elections held in early 2019 secured Buhari his second term and were deemed broadly free and fair. The next election cycle, in 2023, will see two new contenders for the presidency as the Nigerian constitution mandates a two-term presidential limit.

The 2023 elections are likely to be a key moment for young people in Nigeria. This is the moment when it will become visible if the impetus of movements such as #endSARS can be maintained and translated into an electoral force. Some activists are focused on finding young people to stand for leadership positions.

'Sometimes it only takes a few people to change the destiny of a country', says Areo. 'It is the quality of those on the ballot paper where we have a big problem and I feel a few good leaders is what we need to get things done. Student leaders vie for these political spaces in the future. They are what we breed for political spaces. If we can at a grassroots level begin to develop leaders that in ten or seven or five years will sit at the table, we will have a path, a channel, a structure that can change things. It doesn't matter which party they are. If the quality is high, once they get into power, things will change.'

'Since the #endSARS movement the political class are listening, too', says Atang. 'They are thinking about youth participation and youth inclusion, there is a consciousness that they need more youth voices. #endSARS has created more space and more young people want to get involved. We are available, we can do this.'

A key focus for YIAGA Africa is mobilising young voters. 'We have this large cohort of young people between 18 and 25 and the question is how we can help them understand that by voting they are contributing to governance', says Olaniyan. 'It's not just about running for office. Although voting is far away from governance itself, it contributes to good governance.'

Mark Amaza, 33, is senior communications officer at YIAGA Africa. 'If we can somehow get the youth population of Nigeria to participate in politics, I think we can break the system', he says. 'The old are not there in numbers compared to the youth.'

There is hope among activists that 2023 could signal a moment of change. 'I think 2023 is a make-or-break year for us on many levels', says Faruk. 'The president will have run his tenure, so it is an opportunity for a fresh face. And if we can mobilise a mass of young people to come out and vote on election day, I think it's a watershed moment in our history. What we do and the outcomes of 2023 will have a huge impact for the long term.'

The belief that young people can herald a change in how the country is governed is echoed by young people outside Abuja. Nigerian entrepreneur Iyinoluwa Aboyeji, 31, is one of the most successful men of his generation. In conversation he comes across as intelligent, proud, restless, maybe a little impatient. A member of the tech world's global elite – he calls Facebook founder Mark Zuckerberg, 'Zuck' – Aboyeji has presided over several Nigerian companies, including the phenomenally successful online payment system Flutterwave, which he co-founded when he was just 25 and which has a valuation of over US$1 billion.

Aboyeji has now turned his keen mind to shaping the future of his country. 'When I was CEO of Flutterwave, I was starting to see the upper limits of what industry here can achieve because of poor governance so I decided to go and run Madame Oby Ezekwesili's 2019 presidential campaign', he says. 'We made quite a bit of headway, we won the primaries, but ultimately the party that she represented was pushed to endorse another candidate.'

The setback hasn't dented Aboyeji's hopes. 'Nigeria has a very, very young population. There are 26 million people in Nigeria who over the next 10 years are going to turn 18. The largest ever winning presidential election margin in Nigeria was 13 million votes. So even if you only get half of those 18-year-olds to vote for a candidate, that candidate has won.'

Figure 41 Iyinoluwa Aboyeji, 31, is a
technology entrepreneur
Credit: Fati Abubakar

And he has a clear vision for his country. 'Nigeria as the world's greatest Black nation: that's the prize. The dream of building a global Black power has been passed down to us from the very first fathers of liberation until now. And that remains the dream. We want to create a powerful Black nation that can contend with the rest of the world as equals. We can build a great country and stamp our name in the sands of time by creating a Black superpower. That's why we are doing this: so that we can be great, in a great country.'

10 WE'RE IN THIS TOGETHER

'To be young in Nigeria comes with mixed feelings for me. I'm aware of the awesome things young people are doing – talking about tech, talking about art and culture, talking about science – but then the government isn't making things easy. They come up with horrible policies that serve as barriers to the growth of the average young person. They are not helping out in any way. It's frustrating because every young person in Nigeria is doing their best. It's like an abusive relationship – we love our country so much but it's crazy.' Osinachi, 30

'Nigerians are very tenacious and hard-working because there are a lot of things against us. If you can survive in Nigeria, you can survive anywhere. I think of myself over the last 10 years and imagine if I was in a space where we didn't have electricity issues and when you want to start a business, they don't put a lot of tax and regulations. Housing is expensive, it's hard to live a decent life. But people go through all this and still manage to build lives for themselves. I think our situation has strengthened us. We push on regardless. We are young, we are not like our parents' generation, where you can shut us down. My dream is to put Nigeria in the forefront, to help people understand that we have people here who are amazing animators, amazing designers, to export Nigerian talent, to make them see us. That's the future I want to see.' Bolanle, 28

'Honestly, I don't know how it will be. I don't like to be pessimistic but disposable income is shrinking daily as inflation on the price of food rises. What you could buy for 10,000 naira *two months ago has been basically cut in half. The currency crisis is weakening the naira. In 2015, the dollar to the naira was about 150; today it is 500. These are very real issues that affect some people more than others. A lot of our population lives on less than a dollar a day. They are living in extreme poverty and those people know the challenges more than I do. But reiterating that Nigeria has problems doesn't do much good for any of us. I don't feel comfortable saying things won't get better because that's very defeatist and who does it help? We are all in this together and we can only hope that as we move forward, things get better.'* Odunayo, 28

'Nigerians always figure something out. We are the most energetic, lively, hopeful and brightest minds in the world. When we go abroad and see what people in the West complain about, we say, "is that all!" We have much bigger issues to face and we hit the ground running. So, I am hopeful about the future of Nigerians. But there is a survivorship bias to our stories. The people who make it, get the emphasis. We don't hear about the many who didn't. When I was younger, I used to say, "if I can do it, you can", but I know now that my drive and motivation comes from my experiences growing up. It's unfair to expect the same results from someone who had a deprived upbringing. Jesus said: "To whom much is given, much is expected." I have a dream to create a not-for-profit project, a leadership programme that picks young Nigerians with potential and lets them expand their world view. An intensive programme that includes travel and work overseas, so they can learn and then effect change at home. We deserve to be heard in the farthest points of the world. We deserve the right to experience our potential at the highest level. No one can choose the circumstances of their birth and we all deserve opportunity.' John, 34

***

How does it feel to be young in an otherwise ageing world? There are issues, of course, but while things aren't always easy there is real hope. A 2021 intergenerational UNICEF survey found that 57 per cent of young people aged 15 to 24 feel the world is progressing towards a better future.[1] Across the globe, young people are more positive and more globally minded than those over 40. Born into a digital, interconnected and diverse reality, they see a world that is largely a better place than the one their parents grew up in.[2] And it is respondents in the Global South who are the most optimistic about the future, with 69 per cent believing they'd be better off than their parents, compared with just 31 per cent in the Global North.[3]

Young Africans looking to the future confirm this surge of optimism. 'The top line finding in our research is that Africa is not the hell that is so often described', says Kantar West Africa managing director Ndeye Diagne. 'I mean, we live here, we know it's not all bad, but what was mind-blowing for me was how positive overall as a continent we are and how optimistic. Our survey showed people across the continent to be strongly grounded, positive and striving to achieve. There is a real belief that things will keep changing for the better. That is a powerful mindset and I think it is one of our real strengths. If you compare this with Europe or Japan, where less than 30 per cent felt positive about the future, in Africa people are very strong and optimistic. That is the power of Africa. We don't go through life through the prism of the rest of the world.'

In this book you have met a host of young Nigerians, heard their stories and felt their energy and creativity, their self-belief and strength of purpose. The Soro Soke generation is filled with optimism and hope, anger and frustration, drive and ambition. There is a sense that emerges in these conversations that everything is possible. New and transformational forces – including access to technology and growing urbanisation – are reshaping their lifestyles, life choices, economic opportunities, values and culture.

For this generation, being Nigerian and being African has new meaning. Living in urban conurbations that offer a host of opportunities, enabled by their creativity and by the possibility of setting their own narratives, this generation is celebrating its identity and is using music, fashion, literature and film to inspire the rest of the world.

Technology lies at the heart of this cohort's transformation, enabling it to unearth novel solutions to some of the continent's more intractable problems. For young Nigerians, leveraging the Fourth Industrial Revolution is not about copying traditional approaches from the West but conceiving, creating and delivering entirely new, pan-African opportunities. Entrepreneurial at heart, this generation is focused on turning problems into business opportunities and does so with a sense of social justice.

'I like money, it is a very useful tool and I want to make a shit tonne of money. I don't think only arseholes should be billionaires. If I had Bezos' money, there wouldn't be hunger in Africa', says 25-year-old S. I. Ohumu. 'I don't have as much disdain for capitalism as most of my people do. I think there is a way to make money and not destroy the environment. I think there is a way to make money in climate action. There is a lot of money to be made from helping people live in liveable cities. We all progress, when we all progress.'

This cohort evidences a real sense of community. It has a 'we're in this together' mentality, which encompasses everything from improving wealth and opportunity, to accessing power and even breaking down gender stereotypes. 'The rules of happiness in Africa are not the same as elsewhere', says Diagne. 'Community is very strong here and it is more important than material things. There is a saying that the poorest man is not someone who doesn't have money – the poorest man is someone who doesn't have people. Community makes people feel grounded and resilient. It engenders a strong sense of self-belief and helps build new narratives of hope for better and for more.'

Social media is another great enabler, connecting this generation to the rest of the world on an equal footing and helping to engender a pan-African and global mindset. It is also triggering higher expectations. By enabling comparisons with other lives, social media is raising consciousness, highlighting what is no longer tolerable and offering alternatives. Young Nigerians recognise the need for change and social media is empowering them to speak out and realise that change. In the search for equality, greater security and improved prospects, they are using social media to disrupt the status quo and fight for better governance.

This generation stands at the brink of materialising a demographic dividend that is set to change not only the quality of their opportunities but also to reposition the continent's place in global affairs. A technologically, culturally and socially powerful Africa that, far from being an irrelevant corner of the globe, can emerge as a key change-maker of the 21st century. In spending time with young people in the cities of Lagos and Abuja, it quickly becomes clear that they have a bold, positive vision of their country's possibilities. And it is the Soro Soke cohort – children of cities, entrepreneurial creative disruptors who own and solve the problems they've inherited, who use their voices to speak out and all the while celebrate their distinct identity – who will be at the helm.

'I think we have a long way to go but there is hope', says 32-year-old Michael Elégbèdé. 'The tenacity is there, the drive, the desire and the talent and the education. The world has gotten so small. Access to information and access to education is now more available; if you have a cellphone, you have access to research by the best people in the world. Nigerians are intelligent and driven people, and you see all that information and people getting access to it and you see things are happening and you just know that it's going to be amazing. It's a land of opportunity and now those opportunities are becoming so much more vivid and being able to attain them is becoming more real. And we are the focal point of the world right now and I think that's a great thing.'

ACKNOWLEDGEMENTS

So many people helped in creating this book. I owe a particular debt of gratitude to the generosity and assistance of all the people I met in Nigeria, who gave their time, shared their stories and made me feel so welcome. A special thank you to Iyinoluwa Aboyeji, Mark Amaza, Olumide Areo, Kingsley Atang, Yetunde Bakare, Omobolanle Banwo, Odionye Confidence, Ndeye Diagne, Priscilla Eke, Michael Elégbèdé, Odunayo Eweniyi, Ibrahim Faruk, Olumide Idowu, Uyaiedu Ipke-Etim, Tonye Isokariari, Busola Johnson and family, Jude Feranmi, Isaac Matui, Okey Monube, Magnum Muyiwa, Hassan Nurudeen, John Obidi, Rinu Oduala, S. I. Ohumu, Tamara Ojeaga, Davies Okeowo, Chekwube Okonkwo, Fortunes Paul Okoronkwo, Baba Oladeji, Sanusi Olaniyan, Ìfénlá Oligbinde, Chinemerem Onuorah, Osinachi, Funmi Oyatogun, Oyindamola Shoola, Olamide Udoma-Ejorh, Princess Obiajulu Ugwu and Uzor.

A big thank you to all at the Nine Dots Prize for enabling me to follow my passion on this once in a lifetime project and especially to Jane Tinkler, an oasis of calm and a font of good advice. Thanks to Caitlin, James and all at Riot Communications and to everyone at Cambridge University Press, especially Chris Harrison, who always poses interesting questions, also loves Nigeria and is a great walking companion. I am grateful to Maxine Sibihwana for her thoughtful read of and helpful comments on a draft of this book and to Julene Knox for a careful, in-depth edit.

Wolfson College accommodated me in fine style during my time working at the University of Cambridge and the University's Centre for Research in the Arts, Social Sciences and Humanities, fondly known as CRASSH, and especially Stephen, Mette and Michelle, offered me a warm welcome, practical support and an inspiring peek into life at Cambridge. My time in Cambridge was fun as well as productive and that's down to the other research fellows at CRASSH and Wolfson College – thank you for all your moral support, and insightful inputs.

And last but far from least, I want to extend a huge thank you to Kassie Larkins, without whom I would not have found the self-belief to enter the Nine Dots Prize and to Daniel and Diogo for their support, encouragement, ideas and the many glasses of wine they shared with me whenever I was searching for inspiration or in need of reassurance. Thank you all!

NOTES

Chapter 1 The Soro Soke Generation

1 www.thelancet.com/journals/lancet/article/PIIS0140-6736(20)30677-2/fulltext?utm_campaign=gbd20&utm_source=twitter&utm_medium=social
2 https://population.un.org/wpp/
3 www.weforum.org/agenda/2017/04/in-2050-africa-will-be-home-to-1-billion-young-people-and-theyll-need-educating
4 https://mo.ibrahim.foundation/sites/default/files/2020-05/2019-forum-report_0.pdf
5 https://population.un.org/wpp/Publications/Files/WPP2017_KeyFindings.pdf
6 https://population.un.org/wpp/Publications/Files/WPP2017_KeyFindings.pdf
7 www.mckinsey.com/featured-insights/middle-east-and-africa/lions-on-the-move-realizing-the-potential-of-africas-economies
8 www.unfpa.org/sites/default/files/pub-pdf/EN-SWOP14-Report_FINAL-web.pdf
9 www.nytimes.com/2016/03/06/sunday-review/the-world-has-a-problem-too-many-young-people.html
10 www.jstor.org/stable/650179
11 www.newyorker.com/news/daily-comment/black-panther-and-the-invention-of-africa
12 https://population.un.org/wpp/Publications/Files/WPP2017_KeyFindings.pdf
13 www.economist.com/leaders/2021/10/23/insurgency-secessionism-and-banditry-threaten-nigeria
14 www.economist.com/leaders/2021/10/23/insurgency-secessionism-and-banditry-threaten-nigeria

15 www.ft.com/content/ff0595e4-26de-11e8-b27e-cc62a39d57a0

16 https://population.un.org/wpp/

17 www.statista.com/statistics/1121317/age-distribution-of-population-in-nigeria-by-gender/

18 www.weforum.org/agenda/2020/09/the-world-population-in-2100-by-country/

19 www.theparisreview.org/interviews/1720/the-art-of-fiction-no-139-chinua-achebe

20 www.washingtonpost.com/world/interactive/2021/africa-cities/

21 www.washingtonpost.com/world/interactive/2021/africa-cities/

22 www.washingtonpost.com/world/interactive/2021/africa-cities/

23 www.ft.com/content/ff0595e4-26de-11e8-b27e-cc62a39d57a0

24 www.economist.com/leaders/2021/10/23/insurgency-secessionism-and-banditry-threaten-nigeria

25 www.gsma.com/mobileeconomy/sub-saharan-africa/

26 www.brandeins.de/magazine/brand-eins-wirtschaftsmagazin/2021/ballast-abwerfen/unternehmertum-in-afrika-folge-01-der-afrikanische-traum?utm_source=pocket-newtab-global-de-DE

27 www.brandeins.de/magazine/brand-eins-wirtschaftsmagazin/2021/ballast-abwerfen/unternehmertum-in-afrika-folge-01-der-afrikanische-traum?utm_source=pocket-newtab-global-de-DE

Chapter 2 The New York of Nigeria

1 https://worldpopulationreview.com/world-cities/lagos-population

2 www.oecd-ilibrary.org/development/africa-s-urbanisation-dynamics-2020_b6bccb81-en

3 https://mo.ibrahim.foundation/sites/default/files/2021-06/2015-facts-figures_african-urban-dynamics.pdf

4 https://read.oecd-ilibrary.org/development/africa-s-urbanisation-dynamics-2020_b6bccb81-en#page6

5 www.oecd.org/swac/events/africa-urban-realities-february-2020.htm

6   www.sciencedirect.com/science/article/pii/S1574008004800063
7   www.ft.com/content/ff0595e4-26de-11e8-b27e-cc62a39d57a0
8   www.brookings.edu/blog/africa-in-focus/2020/01/21/prerequisites-to-getting-africas-urbanization-right/
9   www.un.org/development/desa/dspd/wp-content/uploads/sites/22/2020/01/World-Social-Report-2020-FullReport.pdf
10 www.economist.com/leaders/2021/10/23/insurgency-secessionism-and-banditry-threaten-nigeria
11 www.reuters.com/article/us-nigeria-economy-poverty-idUSKBN22G19A
12 www.spiegel.de/ausland/lagos-in-nigeria-eine-woche-in-der-chaotischsten-stadt-der-welt-a-69e5f262-a163-45d8-8cf6-15ff7349638b
13 www.spiegel.de/ausland/lagos-in-nigeria-eine-woche-in-der-chaotischsten-stadt-der-welt-a-69e5f262-a163-45d8-8cf6-15ff7349638b
14 www.canvas8.com/content/2020/03/10/gigm-buses.html
15 www.canvas8.com/content/2020/03/10/gigm-buses.html
16 https://journals.openedition.org/cea/116?lang=pt&gathStatIcon=true

Chapter 3 Cultural Capital

1   www.vogue.com.au/fashion/news/why-lagos-is-west-africas-capital-of-culture/image-gallery/62e8f04294c1836348e6950f7f045d0a
2   www.ft.com/content/ff0595e4-26de-11e8-b27e-cc62a39d57a0
3   www.pwc.com/gx/en/entertainment-media/outlook-2020/perspectives.pdf
4   www.pwc.com/gx/en/entertainment-media/outlook-2020/perspectives.pdf
5   https://businesspost.ng/showbiz/nigerias-music-industry-to-generate-n26-3bn-revenue-in-2021-fg/
6   www.researchgate.net/publication/304354533_Urbanization_and_African_Pop_Music_The_Nigerian_Experience

7   www.researchgate.net/publication/304354533_Urbanization_
    and_African_Pop_Music_The_Nigerian_Experience

8   www.redbull.com/int-en/music/the-evolution-of-afropop

9   www.nytimes.com/2020/08/05/arts/music/burna-boy-twice-as-
    tall.html

10 www.kantar.com/campaigns/africa-life-2021

11 www.nytimes.com/2020/08/05/arts/music/burna-boy-twice-as-
    tall.html

12 www.nytimes.com/2020/08/05/arts/music/burna-boy-twice-as-
    tall.html

13 www.nytimes.com/2020/08/05/arts/music/burna-boy-twice-as-
    tall.html

14 www.rollingstone.com/music/music-news/burna-boy-twice-as-
    tall-charts-1049096/

15 www.vogue.com.au/fashion/news/why-lagos-is-west-africas-
    capital-of-culture/image-gallery/62e8f04294c1836348e6950f7f04
    5d0a

Chapter 4 Challenging Norms

1   www.pewresearch.org/fact-tank/2019/04/01/the-countries-with-
    the-10-largest-christian-populations-and-the-10-largest-muslim-
    populations/

2   www.scielo.org.za/scielo.php?script=sci_arttext&pid=S2305-
    445X2015000100010#back_fn1

3   www.scielo.org.za/scielo.php?script=sci_arttext&pid=S2305-
    445X2015000100010#back_fn1

4   www.scielo.org.za/scielo.php?script=sci_arttext&pid=S2305-
    445X2015000100010#back_fn1

5   https://africanarguments.org/2019/08/nigeria-survey-shows-
    decrease-in-homophobic-attitudes-kind-of/

6   https://africanarguments.org/2019/08/nigeria-survey-shows-
    decrease-in-homophobic-attitudes-kind-of/

7   www.academia.edu/49820204/Feminism_is_the_New_Culture_
    for_Nigeria?email_work_card=view-paper

8 www.un.org/africarenewal/news/nigerian-women-say-'no'-gender-based-violence

9 https://afrobarometer.org/sites/default/files/publications/Summary%20of%20results/afrobarometer_sor_nig_r8_en_2021-01-27.pdf

10 https://africanarguments.org/2019/08/nigeria-survey-shows-decrease-in-homophobic-attitudes-kind-of/

11 http://ilo.org/dyn/natlex/natlex4.detail?p_lang=en&p_isn=97399&p_country=NGA&p_count=237

12 https://afrobarometer.org/sites/default/files/publications/Summary%20of%20results/afrobarometer_sor_nig_r8_en_2021-01-27.pdf

13 https://journals.gre.ac.uk/index.php/gswr/article/view/1108/pdf

14 https://journals.gre.ac.uk/index.php/gswr/article/view/1108/pdf

15 www.canvas8.com/content/2020/08/04/nigerian-youth-activism.html

16 https://theface.com/style/orange-culture-nigerian-fashion-menswear-adebayo-oke-lawal-lgbtq-queer-community

17 www.bbc.com/news/world-africa-54070446

18 www.canvas8.com/content/2020/08/04/nigerian-youth-activism.html

19 www.canvas8.com/content/2020/08/04/nigerian-youth-activism.html

Chapter 5 Japá

1 https://mo.ibrahim.foundation/sites/default/files/2020-05/2019-forum-report_0.pdf

2 https://publications.iom.int/system/files/pdf/wmr_2020.pdf

3 https://publications.iom.int/system/files/pdf/wmr_2020.pdf

4 www.tandfonline.com/doi/full/10.1080/10282580.2019.1700368121,DOI:10.1080/10282580.2019.1700368

5 https://mo.ibrahim.foundation/sites/default/files/2020-05/2019-forum-report_0.pdf

6   www.ft.com/content/ca39b445-442a-4845-a07c-0f5dae5f3460

7   https://data.census.gov/cedsci/table?q=place%20of%20
    birth&tid=ACSDT1Y2018.B05006&t=Place%20of%20
    Birth&vintage=2018&hidePreview=true

8   www.ft.com/content/ca39b445-442a-4845-a07c-0f5dae5f3460

9   www.ft.com/content/ca39b445-442a-4845-a07c-0f5dae5f3460

10 https://republic.com.ng/june-july-2021/young-nigerians-search-
    prosperity/

11 https://ec.europa.eu/jrc/sites/default/files/africa_policy_report_
    2018_final.pdf

12 www.un.org/en/development/desa/population/migration/
    publications/migrationreport/docs/MigrationReport2017_
    Highlights.pdf

13 https://publications.iom.int/system/files/pdf/wmr_2020.pdf

14 https://publications.iom.int/system/files/pdf/wmr_2020.pdf

15 https://publications.iom.int/system/files/pdf/wmr_2020.pdf

16 https://reliefweb.int/sites/reliefweb.int/files/resources/
    International%20Migration%202020%20Highlights.pdf
    #page=52

17 www.pwc.com/ng/en/pdf/the-economic-power-of-nigerias-
    diaspora.pdf

18 www.pwc.com/ng/en/pdf/the-economic-power-of-nigerias-
    diaspora.pdf

19 www.youtube.com/watch?v=OqNEhY0crXU

20 www.dw.com/en/stories-of-homecoming-the-young-africans-
    returning-to-the-continent/a-54528478

21 www.dw.com/en/stories-of-homecoming-the-young-africans-
    returning-to-the-continent/a-54528478

Chapter 6 Entrepreneurs with a Mission

1   www.sprinng.org

2   https://hbr.org/2019/12/research-how-technology-could-
    promote-growth-in-6-african-countries

3 www.youthindex.org/country/nigeria
4 www.nigerianstat.gov.ng
5 www.un.org/africarenewal/magazine/january-2021/afcfta-africa-now-open-business
6 www.fdiintelligence.com/article/79638
7 https://journals.sagepub.com/doi/10.1177/0007650315612070
8 www.siemens-stiftung.org/en/media/news/according-to-a-new-siemens-stiftung-study-social-enterprises-are-expected-to-create-much-needed-jobs-in-africa/

Chapter 7 The New Oil

1 https://data.worldbank.org/indicator/IT.NET.USER.ZS?locations=ZG
2 www.statista.com/statistics/1124283/internet-penetration-in-africa-by-country/
3 www.reuters.com/technology/google-invest-1-billion-africa-over-five-years-2021-10-06/
4 www.ifc.org/wps/wcm/connect/6a940ebd-86c6-4a38-8cac-5eab2cad271a/e-Conomy-Africa-2020-Exe-Summary.pdf?MOD=AJPERES&CVID=nmPYAEV
5 https://lagosstate.gov.ng/blog/2021/06/02/lagos-set-to-build-biggest-tech-hub-in-yaba/%20
6 www.ifc.org/wps/wcm/connect/6a940ebd-86c6-4a38-8cac-5eab2cad271a/e-Conomy-Africa-2020-Exe-Summary.pdf?MOD=AJPERES&CVID=nmPYAEV
7 https://africaprudential.com/how-young-africans-are-reinventing-the-future-of-tech-in-africa/
8 www.reuters.com/technology/google-invest-1-billion-africa-over-five-years-2021-10-06/
9 www.berlin-institut.org/en/detail/leapfrogging-africa
10 www.statista.com/statistics/501044/number-of-mobile-cellular-subscriptions-in-nigeria/
11 www.economist.com/graphic-detail/2017/11/08/in-much-of-sub-saharan-africa-mobile-phones-are-more-common-than-access-to-electricity

12 www.gsma.com/mobileeconomy/sub-saharan-africa/

13 www.statista.com/statistics/1124283/internet-penetration-in-africa-by-country/

14 www.statista.com/statistics/467187/forecast-of-smartphone-users-in-nigeria/

15 https://data.gsmaintelligence.com/api-web/v2/research-file-download?id=45121567&file=2794-160719-ME-SSA.pdf

16 https://data.gsmaintelligence.com/api-web/v2/research-file-download?id=45121567&file=2794-160719-ME-SSA.pdf

17 www.imf.org/en/News/Articles/2020/06/15/na061520-digitalizing-sub-saharan-africa-hopes-and-hurdles

Chapter 8 The Hashtag Generation

1 www.bbc.com/news/world-africa-55099016

2 https://edition.cnn.com/videos/world/2020/11/23/nigeria-endsars-cctv-investigation-lon-orig-mkd.cnn

3 www.amnesty.org.uk/press-releases/nigeria-cover-lekki-toll-gate-massacre-continues-100-days-after-killings

4 https://edition.cnn.com/2021/11/15/africa/lekki-tollgate-judicial-panel-report-intl/index.html

5 www.stearsng.com/article/the-political-awakening-of-nigerias-youth

6 https://twitter.com/fisayosoyombo

7 www.theguardian.com/world/2020/oct/06/video-of-nigerian-police-shooting-man-in-street-sparks-outcry

8 https://institute.global/policy/social-media-futures-changing-african-narrative

9 https://mo.ibrahim.foundation/sites/default/files/2020-05/2019-forum-report_0.pdf

10 https://africanarguments.org/2021/10/africas-revolution-will-be-tweeted-if-activists-can-harness-the-opportunity/

11 https://africanarguments.org/2021/10/africas-revolution-will-be-tweeted-if-activists-can-harness-the-opportunity/

12 www.notion.so/ec69f91c9acd4582b72c0a6fa11d8d09?
v=811277be749e44468a23203924129266
13 www.nendo.co.ke/post/endsars-analyzing-48-million-tweets-in-
10-days-using-brandwatch
14 https://mg.co.za/africa/2021-04-27-how-youth-can-reshape-
political-participation-in-nigeria/
15 https://africanarguments.org/2021/10/africas-revolution-will-be-
tweeted-if-activists-can-harness-the-opportunity/
16 https://mo.ibrahim.foundation/sites/default/files/2020-05/2019-
forum-report_0.pdf
17 https://edition.cnn.com/2021/11/15/africa/lekki-tollgate-judicial-
panel-report-intl/index.html
18 https://mg.co.za/africa/2021-04-27-how-youth-can-reshape-
political-participation-in-nigeria/

Chapter 9 Contesting for Power

1 https://mo.ibrahim.foundation/sites/default/files/2020-05/2019-
forum-report_0.pdf
2 https://africanarguments.org/2018/03/young-people-are-not-just-
the-future-of-nigeria-they-are-nigeria-today-not-too-young-to-run/
3 https://mo.ibrahim.foundation/sites/default/files/2020-05/2019-
forum-report_0.pdf
4 www.economist.com/leaders/2021/10/23/insurgency-
secessionism-and-banditry-threaten-nigeria
5 https://theconversation.com/why-buharis-government-is-losing-
the-anti-corruption-war-155488
6 www.premiumtimesng.com/news/headlines/265484-buhari-
criticises-nigerian-youth-as-lazy-uneducated.html
7 www.cddwestafrica.org https://www.cddwestafrica.org/how-
youth-can-reshape-political-participation-in-nigeria/
8 https://mo.ibrahim.foundation/sites/default/files/2020-05/2019-
forum-report_0.pdf
9 https://mo.ibrahim.foundation/sites/default/files/2020-05/2019-
forum-report_0.pdf

10 https://mo.ibrahim.foundation/sites/default/files/2020-05/2019-forum-report_0.pdf

11 www.canvas8.com/content/2019/09/13/nigeria-youth-culture.html

12 www.canvas8.com/content/2020/08/04/nigerian-youth-activism.html

13 https://blogs.lse.ac.uk/africaatlse/2019/11/27/nigerian-youths-poor-political-office-activism/

14 https://blogs.lse.ac.uk/africaatlse/2019/11/27/nigerian-youths-poor-political-office-activism/

15 https://blogs.lse.ac.uk/africaatlse/2019/11/27/nigerian-youths-poor-political-office-activism/

16 https://blogs.lse.ac.uk/africaatlse/2019/11/27/nigerian-youths-poor-political-office-activism/

17 https://blogs.lse.ac.uk/africaatlse/2019/11/27/nigerian-youths-poor-political-office-activism/

Chapter 10 We're in This Together

1 https://changingchildhood.unicef.org/stories/future-fortunes

2 https://changingchildhood.unicef.org/stories/future-fortunes

3 https://changingchildhood.unicef.org/stories/future-fortunes

Printed in the United States
by Baker & Taylor Publisher Services